PSL MO

RAILWAY GUIDE

3

Structure Modelling

Michael Andress

Patrick Stephens, Cambridge

First published in 1980

Also in the same series and by the same author

1 Baseboards, track and electrification
2 Layout Planning
4 Scenery

In preparation

5 Operating your layout
6 Branchline railways
7 Modern railways
8 Narrow gauge railways

British Library Cataloguing in Publication Data

Andress, Michael
Model railway guide.
3: Structures
1. Railroads—Models
I. Title
625.1'9 TF197

ISBN 0 85059 400 6

Cover photograph by Brian Monaghan showing a member of the Macclesfield Model Railway Society.

Text photoset in 8 on 9pt Univers by Manuset Limited, Baldock, Herts.
Printed in Great Britain on 90 gsm Pedigree coated cartridge and bound by The Garden City Press, Letchworth, for the publishers Patrick Stephens Limited, Bar Hill, Cambridge, CB3 8EL, England.

Contents

Introduction

The construction of model buildings can be a very enjoyable pastime. While architectural modelling is an important part of the professional modelmaker's work, most amateurs only become involved indirectly, usually through railway modelling. At one time the only buildings to be found on a model railway layout were essential railway structures such as stations, goods sheds, signal boxes and bridges, and these were often unrealistic, toy-like items. Now, however, the landscape which provides the setting for a model railway has become much more important and there has been a marked improvement in the scope and standard of both scenic and structure modelling in an effort to achieve greater realism.

The steadily increasing interest in this aspect of the hobby has led to the commercial production of kits of various types and there is now a range available which is excellent in both extent and quality, particularly in 00, HO and N scales. There have also been a number of new materials and techniques applied to scratch-building which have brought about an increase in realism. The standards are now high with the best structure models being remarkably accurate, realistic and well detailed.

My aim in this book is to indicate to the beginner what is available and to give him or her some ideas on how to utilise effectively the many kits, parts and different materials in building structures for a model railway layout. I include both sexes in the last sentence quite deliberately as this is a facet of railway modelling which the ladies often especially enjoy and which they tackle very successfully! Though the examples will be mainly relevant to railway modelling, many of the kits, materials and construction techniques are equally suitable for military modelling and wargaming, fields in which there is now considerable interest in building structure models for inclusion in settings for military figures, tanks, guns and vehicles. Bus modellers may also want to construct buildings as these vehicles are often displayed on large or small layouts or dioramas, a bus depot being a favourite choice of subject. I have also seen interesting ship model displays where the vessels are shown in a harbour, dock or shipyard setting with appropriate structures completing the scene. Aircraft models are sometimes displayed on dioramas which include buildings—a small airfield being a good example. Tramway layouts usually need numerous structures as such models are typically set in town or city surroundings. Last, but not least, there are those modellers whose primary interest is in architectural work. Thus, the scope for structure modelling is considerable.

This book concentrates mainly on the most popular railway modelling scales, 00, HO and N, though some examples from other scales are aiso included. However, some of the information relating to kits and all the scratch-building data can be applied to most scales used in modelling structures.

I would like to thank all those modellers who have helped me with photographs and information for this book. In particular I am grateful to Graham Bailey, Tony Butler, Olive Clark, Howard Coulson, Steven Dewhirst, Allan Downes, Roy England, Len Fidkin, Keith Gowen, P.D. Hancock, Trevor Hughes, Terry Jenkins, Bob Jones, Betty Kay, The Middlesbrough Model Railway and Tramway Club, Dave Rowe, George Sellios, Doris Stokes and Colin Woolridge. I am also grateful to those manufacturers who have assisted me with information and pictures of their products.

Some basic points

As there are relatively few ready-made structure models available, though Grafar and Bachmann offer N-scale ranges, most beginners start their model making with a few structure kits, often to add to a train set or a small and simple first scale layout. Such kit models are an excellent introduction because they are generally easy and quick to build and they provide useful experience in constructional work. As they are usually static items they need only look attractive and accuracy in assembly is less important than for models such as locomotives and rolling stock which must run well to be successful. Mistakes or poor finishing in the original construction can often be improved by a little extra work later when the modeller has gained in experience and skill. Alternatively if the first attempts are completely unsuccessful they can be discarded or put into the scrap box as a source of parts for other buildings without much loss as the kits are, on the whole, not very expensive. The knowledge and practice gained with structure modelling will be of benefit for other aspects of the hobby and the successful completion of a few small and simple building kits can do much to boost the confidence and interest in the tackling of more difficult projects.

As I have already implied, the beginner is most likely to find enjoyment and success in structure modelling by starting with something simple. Choose a fairly small and easy-to-build card or plastic kit first, then progress to larger and more complex kits, trying all the time to make each model better than the one before both in neatness of construction and in the finishing. Ideas for extra detailing and then for alterations and conversions from the basic kits will soon come once you get started. Once some skill in kit assembly and conversion has been achieved there is no reason why the modeller should not build from scratch if he or she wishes. For a first attempt at scratch-building there is much to be said for following one of the many articles which appear in the modelling magazines describing the construction of various types of buildings. Such an article will provide all the prototype information needed as well as detailed instructions on how the model can be made. You will find it of value to read as many of these articles as you can,

Below and over page *Two views of the remarkable city model, based on London, constructed in 1 mm scale by Norman Clark. The trains and road vehicles move on endless belts and the model is also lit for viewing as a night scene. The buildings have been constructed largely from card.*

even though you do not plan to build the actual models described, as you will learn much about the methods of construction which can be used. The knowledge you acquire in this way can then be applied to the modelling of buildings which do interest you. Quite often you will find that the authors of these articles have made improvements to conventional construction methods or have devised new techniques and these may help you in your own modelling by making construction easier or the results more realistic.

Unless you are an architectural modeller, and perhaps not even then, you will not be making single models of buildings to be displayed individually, but a number of structures to be placed together on a model railway layout or a diorama of some type. Thus the choice of models, whether kits or scratch-built, must be judged not only by their suitability as regards your skill and experience and their individual appeal but also in relation to the overall effect required. This selection is essential if you are to achieve a realistic appearance for your layout as a whole, and it does require care and thought. You will also need to be able to resist the temptation to acquire models you like but which are unsuitable for the scene you are planning!

Ideally your layout, even if not a model of a particular prototype line, should be based in a more or less specific geographical location and the buildings chosen should be appropriate in architectural style and in the materials, such as brick, stone or wood, used in construction. If your layout is to be a period model, care must be taken to avoid introducing anachronisms. The different structures should also blend in well together though this is more difficult to assess in advance, particularly for the beginner, unless a group of structures from a prototype setting are reproduced together. The railway buildings of a particular region or railway company often have a characteristic style and it is important to model this correctly if the right effect is to be produced. In real towns and villages there is often considerable variation in style and period between the buildings, with new concrete and glass office blocks next to timbered houses and so on. However, in model form we must be a little cautious in what we copy, selecting, as an artist may in painting a picture, the best features and omitting those which would spoil the scene. This is important because of the compression we must carry out in modelling a town or village on a small layout and because we get an overall view of the model rather than just seeing part at a time as we do when walking along a real street. Thus we must try to create a somewhat idealised or representational scene with the character and atmosphere of the prototype rather than an exact copy. Some of our most successful scenic and structure modellers, John Ahern, P.R. Wickham, and P.D. Hancock, for example, have created detailed historical and geographical backgrounds for the imaginary

Opposite page *Three views of an 009 narrow-gauge layout constructed by the Middlesbrough Model Railway and Tramway Club. The railway buildings and mine have been scratch-built with similar architectural styles and construction materials giving a harmonious appearance which adds much to the realism and atmosphere of the layout. Note the unusual, but prototypical, water tank by the engine shed.*

TIME TABLE
WOLF'S RAKE
2
12

This footbridge at Market Redwing station on Keith Gowen's TT-scale layout is a Triang model which has been modified to give it a more characteristic GWR appearance.

prototypes on which their layouts were modelled. While these modellers obviously gained enjoyment from this I realise that many others would not be interested in such a digression from their practical modelling. Even so the results are likely to be much better if the modeller is prepared to give a little consideration at the beginning to the background for his layout. He can then choose appropriate structures and will have some idea of what he is trying to achieve as far as the overall appearance is concerned.

The arrangement of the model structures is also important in the creation of a realistic and visually effective grouping on the layout or diorama. You may be uncertain at first how to obtain this but you will find that a little experimentation and practice will help. It is also valuable to think about groupings, either of real buildings or of models on layouts built by the experts, and to decide why they are effective. There is much to be said for planning all the structures for your layout at an early stage, rather than adding them piecemeal, as this will give you more chance of creating a well-composed scene. A useful technique is to make from scrap card rough mock-up models of the structures you plan to have. These shapes can be tried in various positions and groupings until the most satisfactory is determined. You may find that some modification to one or more of the buildings will be advantageous or that one of the structures cannot be fitted in successfully. It is, of course,

Beautifully modelled farm buildings in 4 mm scale by Allan Downes. The structures have been grouped to make an interesting and attractive scene. (Photograph by John Priest.)

Natural grouping adds to the realism and effectiveness of these superb 4 mm scale models scratch-built by Allan Downes. Note the accurately modelled stone walling and the creeper on the wall of the cottages. (Photograph by John Priest.)

much better to find this out before you actually build the models! Some of the kit catalogues provide the dimensions for each of the models in the range and this will also be helpful for the modeller in advance planning before purchasing the kits. The structures should obviously be planned in conjunction with the scenery to provide the most effective setting for a model railway.

Incidentally, the architectural models built by the professionals are worthy of study because great care is taken to present these in the most visually effective way possible. After all the appearance may make the difference between winning or missing out on an important contract! Study these models carefully and you will often pick up useful ideas for your own layout.

As there is space on most model railway layouts for only a limited number of buildings we should be selective and choose only interesting and attractive structures, each of which will add to the overall appearance. If they are not to dwarf the rest of the layout and if we are to have enough buildings to provide interesting variety, our structures should be small. By this I do not mean that they should be underscale, though this can be useful for background models as we shall see later, but that we should select small prototypes. Generally these structures will also be more appropriate to the scope of the railway facilities, the number and length of sidings and so on, which we will have space for on a layout. However, you may find an interesting subject you would like to model but which would be too large for your layout if copied exactly. It is often possible by applying what has been called 'selective compression' to such a building to retain the original character while significantly reducing the size of the model. Industrial buildings such as factories and warehouses are often made up of a number of repeated similar or identical units or sections and some of these can be omitted to make the model smaller. A three-storey structure can be cut down to two, the number of doors and windows can be reduced, windows can be made smaller and closer together, and chimneys and skylights can similarly be reduced in size. However, the height of doors and of loading platforms should not be altered and the clearances for any openings through which railway rolling stock passes must, of couse, be maintained. Using these techniques it should be possible to reduce the size of a structure to about two thirds of the linear dimensions and this will cut down the ground area to approximately a third, an appreciable saving.

For buildings in the background and away from the tracks so that they will not be compared directly to the size of the locomotives and rolling stock, a reduction can be made simply by modelling to a smaller scale. In

Above *Typical of the superb architectural models produced professionally is this one of a Middle Eastern army barracks built by Thorp Modelmakers Ltd of London. The amateur will benefit from studying work of this type.* (Photograph by courtesy of Thorp Modelmakers.)

Below *The choice of prototype is important in an effective model. The rock bunker on which this HO-scale Fine Scale Miniatures kit was based is an excellent subject with its interesting lines and many surface details such as the wood framing, the stairway and the conveyor belts. Note the shelter over the railroad track with the fully detailed corrugated iron roof. This superb craftsman wood kit includes many cast metal detailing items and is complete except for the figures shown in this picture.* (Photograph by courtesy of Fine Scale Miniatures.)

The small size of N-scale models may allow relatively large industries to be featured on a model railway layout. Graham Bailey constructed this realistic ship-building and repair yard, complete with a ship being built, for his modern British prototype layout. The ship is a modified Novo 'Shell Welder' kit and the gantry crane in the background is a cut down Pola HO-scale kit model. The rest of the structures were scratch-built.

most cases the modeller uses a scale only slightly smaller, for example $\frac{1}{8}$ in to the foot on an 00 or HO-scale layout. However, this can be taken much further to give the impression of great depth to a scene, even though there are only a few inches of actual distance available in front of the backscene, by forcing the perspective. This is similar to the way an artist uses perspective drawing to make his two-dimensional picture appear to have depth as well. It is a technique which is extensively, and expertly, employed in museum dioramas and you can see examples in many museums, for example, the Science Museum in London. It has not been much used by railway modellers, partly because the viewpoint must be rather strictly limited for the most successful results and this cannot usually be achieved on an ordinary model railway layout. However, the late Jack Nelson applied perspective modelling most effectively in a number of superb dioramas of the LNWR, and I believe there are plans for these models to be put on public show. The subject is rather beyond the scope of this book and I would refer readers to an article by Mr Nelson in the November 1971 issue of *Model Railways* magazine for more information. I can, however, give an example of how forced perspective can be applied simply but effectively on a layout. At a branch line terminus there may be a street running along behind the station, parallel to and a few inches in front of the backdrop. The houses or shops along this street are modelled to full scale for 00. Running back from this street towards the backdrop, but curving round, is another road. The buildings on this are constructed as if drawn in perspective, with the end nearest the viewer higher than the end away from the onlooker. This can be quite marked with the scale going from 00 at the front to N scale at the rear in only a couple of buildings. Positioning figures of appropriate scale in relation to the front and rear structures enhances the effect. Any features in these distorted walls must also be modelled in the same way, for example, doors, windows and so on. Making the road curve round so that it goes out of sight behind the other buildings avoids the need to continue the perspective on the drawn backscene, a task which may prove difficult unless the modeller has some artistic skill. Because the road runs back the viewpoint is relatively limited to more or less in front, thus helping to overcome one of the problems with perspective modelling. It is important, however, to view the scene from close to model ground level for the best effect. Looking down from above will distort the appearance. The buildings on the rear of the curve can be modelled as low relief structures (see later), as well as in perspective, to save space.

Sources of ideas and information

The beginner can learn a great deal by reading the model railway magazines and books and by looking at photographs appearing there of layouts built by experienced modellers. Often the techniques employed in construction are described and study of the pictures also helps in understanding how these workers have achieved realistic arrangements and groupings and the all-important 'atmosphere'. Many kit conversions have been described in the model press and following one of these can be a good introduction to this type of work. These conversions will also give you ideas for other, original modifications of your own. Visits to model railway exhibitions will prove very helpful as well as most enjoyable. Provided you choose a moment when they are not too busy operating to talk to members of the public you will find that most exhibitors are very willing to answer questions about how they built the models on their layouts and to explain any construction techniques which they use. Membership of a club can also be very beneficial as you can learn a great deal from the more experienced members. Not only will they advise you on how to build your models and give you practical assistance too if necessary, but they can also help you to avoid the mistakes they have made in the past!

Museum models and dioramas are worthy of study as they will give you ideas on the most effective methods of presentation, particularly regarding aspects such as perspective modelling and lighting. A visit to the Pendon Museum is especially recommended. Not only can you see what must be some of the finest structure modelling ever carried out in 4 mm scale in the Pendon Parva village (some pictures of which are included in this book) and other displays, but also John Ahern's famous 'Madder Valley' layout which is on permanent loan to the museum.

For scratch-building, many photographs and plans of railway and other suitable structures appear in the model railway magazines and there are also articles detailing the construction of various models. As I mentioned earlier a good approach for the beginner is to build at least one model based on an article of this type before going on to choose his own prototypes

A scene at Madderport on John Ahern's famous 00-scale 'Madder Valley' model railway layout, now on display at the Pendon Museum. The buildings were constructed from card and were based on real structures; the building at the left of the photograph, for example, is a model of the harbour office at Poole, Dorset. Note the low relief structures at the rear of the layout. (Photograph by courtesy of Pendon Museum.)

Some of the buildings from the 4 mm scale Pendon Parva village model at Pendon Museum. The structures, which are all accurate replicas of real buildings, are built to the highest museum standards and the degree of detailing is almost unbelievable. Construction is mainly from card while the windows are glazed with either real glass, microscope cover slips, or mica. Thatching was carried out with human hair but tow is now used. The interiors are fully modelled. (Photographs by courtesy of Pendon Museum.)

to model. A few plans are available commercially. The Skinley range includes some structures, while MAP have a selection of plans in 4 mm scale for buildings designed by John Ahern. Many pictures of prototypes are to be found in books and magazines, on picture postcards and so on, and these can all be useful. It is a good idea to build up a file of pictures of structures and details of buildings which interest you so that you can use them for reference purposes in your modelling.

Best of all is to go out and look for buildings you would like to model. You will be surprised how interesting and enjoyable a stroll around an industrial, railway, dock or other area can be when you have such a purpose. If possible take a pencil and notebook, a camera, and perhaps a tape-measure with you and make notes and sketches, take numerous pictures and keep a record of a few basic dimensions for any buildings which you like. It is also useful to collect information on small details which you can model, even if the structure as a whole is not suitable. Modelling such features accurately will add authenticity and realism to your model buildings. Industrial structures in particular often have a great deal in the way of pipes, tanks, valves, ventilators, ducts, extractor fans and so on visible on the exterior and adding appropriate features to your models will make them more interesting. There is no need to model any building exactly as it is unless you wish to, and you will often find that you would like to make alterations to suit your own ideas and to meet the requirements of your layout more closely. Sometimes combining features from several different prototypes may result in the most suitable building for your scene.

If you are one of those lucky people who can sketch well this will be very useful in collecting information on prototypes. Even if your drawing is not good you can still make rough sketches which can be adequate as a record, especially if you keep them fairly simple and if you note down enough dimensions from which to model accurately. Personally I find photography the most convenient method and I take my camera with me whenever I think I may be somewhere that there may be buildings of interest. I document any structure of interest photographically, when I have the opportunity, even if the information does not seem to be of immediate use. I may want to refer to it in the future and I also find that a look through my file often gives me ideas for modelling projects. As black and white film is cheap it is worth while taking plenty of pictures. Straight on views of the front, sides and back are useful for modelling purposes and, if you can show a person of known height in the pictures, this will help you in estimating the dimensions and will usually enable you to draw up a sufficiently accurate plan from which to build a model. Though the film is more expensive it is also a good idea to take some colour pictures if possible as this will be helpful when you come to paint the model. Even if you do not follow the original colour scheme the pictures will be a good guide to weathering.

If you do take a considerable number of pictures it is desirable to have some form of filing which will permit convenient storage and retrieval of any particular negative. I take mainly 35 mm films and I store the negatives in Paterson and Photo Science negative files which are loose-leaf folders holding separate sheets each of which will take a 36 exposure 35 mm film cut into strips of six pictures. Before filing the negatives I contact print each film on to a sheet of 10 in × 8 in enlarging paper in a Paterson contact printer. The contact sheet for each film is then filed with the loose leaf holding that film. This makes it easier to locate the negative for a particular picture but ideally the negatives should also be cross indexed according to subject. A simple method is to give each sheet a number and also each negative, for example 10/18 would be the 18th negative on sheet 10. File cards are made up for different subjects, for example, signal boxes, and filed alphabetically. The relevant negative numbers are then listed on the cards together with further brief identifying notes.

Industrial structures are often interesting in model form. This attractive processing plant is a source of extra traffic on P.D. Hancock's well-known 4 mm scale narrow-gauge 'Craig & Mertonford Railway' layout. The model was scratch-built from card, stripwood and corrugated copper sheet. (Photograph by P.D. Hancock.)

Tools

Relatively few tools are needed for structure modelling and the beginner can easily and inexpensively assemble a suitable selection. My tool kit contains the following items.

Modelling knife I use Swann Morton knives but the X-Acto ones are equally suitable. Both are of the type with replaceable blades and both manufacturers offer a range of different blade shapes for varying purposes. I find it convenient to have two handles and to fit a new blade in one. As this blade becomes less sharp I transfer it to the other handle and fit another new one to the first. The handles are marked appropriately and I can use the sharper blade for fine work and the other for rougher jobs. Always fit a new blade when embarking on any delicate or difficult work as you will find it much easier to get good results with a really sharp knife. For heavier work I use a Stanley knife. This again has replaceable blades but both the knife and the blades are of sturdier construction then the Swann Morton ones, making it useful for cutting thicker material.

Razor saw This is very useful for cutting thicker plastic sheet and thick kit parts as well as wood strip and sheet. I use an X-Acto saw handle with replaceable blades, but other makes are also available. The X-Acto Mitre Box designed for use with the saw is very convenient for cutting right angles and 45-degree angles.

Steel rule and steel square These are required for accurate measuring and marking out and I always use a steel rule as a guide for cutting with a modelling knife. It is handy to have a 6 in rule for small parts and a 12 or 18 in one for longer cuts.

Scriber This can be used for marking out and is also good for scribing planking on plastic, card or wood. An alternative is to use a needle held in a pin vice.

Pin vice This, with a selection of fine drills, enables me to make small holes for fixing small details on to structure models.

Hand drill This is used with drills too large for the pin vice when larger holes are required.

Fine files I have a set of needle files of different shapes, round, square, flat, oval, half round and triangular and these are very useful for a variety of tasks including smoothing, shaping, enlarging openings and so on.

Fine sandpaper This is also essential for smoothing and finishing.

Tweezers These are needed for handling small parts and I have two pairs, one coarse and one fine with pointed tips.

Scissors These are useful for cutting out parts especially along curved or irregular lines which may be more difficult with a knife. I have several pairs including one very fine pair suitable for very delicate work.

Small clothes pegs These are extremely useful for all sorts of holding jobs in model making. Bulldog clips and rubber bands are also good for this purpose. Uses for these items include keeping parts together and correctly aligned while glue is setting, holding parts while you cut, file or sand them and holding small items while they are painted and until the paint dries.

Small vice This is also used to hold parts and materials while they are cut or shaped.

Fine pliers These are employed for various jobs particularly for bending wire and metal when modelling piping and other details.

Wood burning tool This tool is intended for burning decorative designs on wood but it can also be used to model stone, brick and various types of wood planking by burning appropriately placed grooves into sheet balsa. The model I have can also be used as a soldering iron. The Pyrogravure, popular with military modellers, who use it to achieve a variety of effects in plastic, is a similar but rather more sophisticated and controllable piece of equipment.

Soldering iron This is not often needed for structure modelling but is sometimes useful in making details such as handrails, piping and so on.

Painting equipment will be discussed in a later section.

Board A surface on which to work and cut is

essential. I often use chipboard or hardboard as they have no grain to catch the knife blade and direct it away from the line of the cut. The hardboard needs replacing fairly frequently as the surface quickly becomes marked, but it is inexpensive. If you do use hardboard always work on the smooth face. Some modellers recommend glass as a working surface but this has the disadvantage of being breakable and it also tends to blunt the knife blades quickly.

The tools I have listed above are ones which I have found useful but they are by no means essential for all structure modelling. If you build only from pre-cut card kits for example it is possible to get by with almost no tools at all. Conversely you may find items which I have not listed are useful to you in your modelling. Always be on the lookout for tools which can be employed to help in your construction work as you can come across some surprisingly useful items quite unexpectedly, particularly now so many tools are available for do-it-yourself work.

It is, of course, important to take care of your tools and to store them when not in use so that they do not become broken or blunted. It is also much easier to find the particular item you need if your tools are kept neat and tidy.

Last, but not least, it is essential to learn to hold and use your tools correctly. Not only will your work be better, with less likelihood of damaging the tools, but even more important you will not run the risk of injury as you may if you use them incorrectly. Make sure whenever you are cutting, sawing, drilling or filing that if the tool should slip it will not reach your hands. If possible hold parts in a vice if they are small or difficult to hold by hand while you are working on them.

You will find that your modelling is better and more enjoyable if you have good working conditions. I find it most comfortable to work at a table or desk sitting on a chair of appropriate height. As one may spend a whole evening at work on a model a good position will make neck or backache less likely. Perhaps most often overlooked is the importance of good lighting, arranged so that you are not working in your own shadow. When marking out and cutting you must be able to see well if you are to do accurate work. Poor lighting also leads to eyestrain, headaches and tiredness, none of which is conducive to enjoyable or successful modelling! I find an Anglepoise type of lamp ideal as this can be adjusted to exactly the right position for whatever I am doing. When using some model cements and solvents you should ensure that there is good ventilation and that you are not inhaling excessive amounts of vapour. It is not advisable to smoke when using these chemicals.

Materials

The materials you use will be influenced by the type of modelling you are doing and perhaps the construction materials employed for the prototype you are following, but also by your own personal preferences. Modellers, being inventive and imaginative people, have tried many different raw materials for scratch-building and for detailing and conversion work on kit models. The following list includes most of those commonly used and the beginner will find it advantageous to try out a variety of these before deciding which he will utilise for his models.

Card This is the traditional material for model building construction and is still the choice of several of the experts despite the introduction of plastic card. It is generally best to buy good quality card as the extra cost will not be very great for the relatively small quantities required. Smooth-surfaced card in different thicknesses and in a variety of colours can be purchased at art shops. For interior floors and bracing, cheaper quality card can be used if desired but this should be fairly thick and strong.

Balsa wood This light, soft wood is available in model and toy shops as blocks, sheets and strips of varying sizes. It is easy to cut and shape and is useful for floors, internal bracing and for walls which are to be faced with some other material. It is also useful for models of buildings of timber construction and for trestle bridges, though the surface texture and grain are rather too coarse.

Hard wood Some British model shops stock obechi stripwood in various sizes and this is useful for timber buildings. The larger sizes of stripwood can also often be obtained from DIY shops and can be employed for interior bracing. In the United States a wide range of sizes of bass is available including very small sizes and also a variety of sections such as T, L, H and I girders. Sheetwood machined to represent planking, capped siding, lapboard siding and so on, is also produced. These materials are marketed in Britain by some of the specialist shops such as Victors of Islington.

Drawing paper This is available in a variety of thicknesses and surface finishes from art shops and has many uses including modelling slates, tiles, individually applied bricks and stones.

Plastic card This is sheet polystyrene in a range of thicknesses and in various colours

Superb scratch-building in 2 mm scale by Len Fidkin. This oil derrick model was constructed following an article by American modeller George Allen in Model Railroader *magazine in September 1952. The model was made almost entirely from wood.*

This prize-winning 2 mm scale American trestle bridge was scratch-built by Len Fidkin using fine stripwood.

including white and black. It is very easy to cut, using a modelling knife for the thinner sheets and a razor saw for the thicker material. Shaping is also easy with files and sandpaper and the finish is very good with no grain visible. Plastic card models can be assembled using solvent adhesives which are very convenient to use. These qualities have made this material very popular with modellers and it is widely used in scratch-building structure models. It can also be used very satisfactorily in carrying out conversions of plastic kits. Plastic card is also sold as fine strips of various sizes, and this is very handy when quantities of fine strip are needed for a model as it saves a great deal of cutting. Clear plastic sheet is produced for glazing windows. Plastic card is also made in embossed sheets for representing brick, stone course and random stone, cobblestones and so on, in various scales. When appropriately painted the effect is very good as the embossing provides a realistic relief to the surface.

Plastic shapes Plastruct offer a wide range of girders, rods, tubes, beams and many other shapes for various scales made in ABS plastic. These parts were originally marketed for professional workers constructing models of industrial installations but are now available also for amateur modellers. Fine plastic rod is made by various manufacturers.

Plastic filler Used to fill gaps and holes in plastic before finishing and painting and also useful for making alterations in plastic kits. Suitable fillers are made by several manufacturers including Humbrol. Milliput make a useful two part epoxy filler.

Expanded polystyrene This light foam plastic is easy to work and is quite strong. It can be used for constructing model building walls, stone walling and so on. This material is sold at DIY shops either as sheets of varying thicknesses or as ceiling tiles but large quantities are used as packing and you may be able to obtain this material as scrap without cost. Expanded polystyrene can be dangerous if inhaled so care should be taken when working with it, particularly if you are sawing or filing it.

Brick, stone, slate and tile paper These papers, printed in colour, are produced in the main small scales by various manufacturers including Builder Plus and Superquick. Faller make a range of thicker printed materials which have the pattern embossed for greater realism.

Corrugated metal This represents corrugated iron sheeting on model buildings. Slaters make corrugated copper sheet for this

Above *The late Eric Kay built this impressive viaduct for his N-scale 'Sherrington Branch' using polystyrene foam sawn and carved to shape.*

Below *Eitomo station building on Howard Coulson's 'N & M R' an 009 layout closely based on East African narrow-gauge railways. The model was scratch-built after study of photographs of prototype stations. Corrugated iron walls and roof were represented by corrugated copper sheet.*

purpose. In the United States Campbell Scale Models market thin corrugated aluminium sheet which is exact scale for HO and very realistic in appearance. You may be able to obtain this from specialist shops in Britain.

Plaster A material which has been used very effectively in structure modelling particularly for stone-walled prototypes. Either ordinary hardwall plaster or dental plaster can be employed. Plaster fillers such as Polyfilla and Tapwata are also useful in modelling buildings.

Das This is a type of modelling clay which has been used successfully in modelling stonework.

Kos (Pyruma) A fire cement which can be used in structure modelling.

Peco texture modelling compound A modelling material with a variety of applications in model building construction.

Perspex Buildings with large and numerous windows can be conveniently built from perspex with overlays of thin card or plastic card cut out to reveal the perspex beneath where the windows are to be.

Glass Some modellers like to use real glass, usually microscope cover slips, for windows in model buildings.

Miscellaneous There are innumerable odds and ends which can be employed in modelling, especially for detailing purposes on industrial buildings. Many are things which are being discarded and so will not cost you anything! As you become more experienced in detailing, converting and scratch-building you will find that you develop the knack of seeing the modelling potential in many apparently unlikely objects, though you must be careful not to get too good at it or you will be reluctant ever to throw anything away, an attitude which is not generally popular with other members of the household!

Wire of varying thicknesses can be used as ducts, piping, handrails, bracing wires, cables and so on, while staples are convenient for modelling grab-irons. Old toothpaste tubes opened out provide a supply of thin, easy-to-work metal from which pieces of corrugated iron, metal covers and other details can be fabricated. Old, broken toys and domestic utensils often provide useful bits and pieces as do old plastic kit models.

As with your tools, the materials and parts you have in stock should be stored neatly to avoid damage and also to enable you to find what you are looking for quickly and easily. For the storage of small items I bought several inexpensive sets of plastic parts storage drawers from a local DIY shop. These are very convenient as they can be stacked up on top of each other against a wall and so do not require much space. As the drawers are transparent it is possible to get some idea of where things are even without opening them, but I have also added labels for extra convenience.

Kits and kit construction

There is now a very wide range of kits of various types and materials, particularly in the most popular railway modelling scales.

Card kits These offer the largest selection of British prototype structures. The standard material for scratch-building is card, usually covered with brick- or stone-paper. By using good-quality card, printed in full colour, the manufacturers offer the modeller convenience in construction with an excellent finished appearance.

The Hamblings Bilteezi range was first introduced in 1948 and was later expanded. There is a good range of railway and other buildings in 00 scale and a smaller selection in TT. There was also an N-scale series but only two of these are still available, one being the row of low relief suburban shops shown in one of the accompanying pictures. The windows on the Bilteezi sheets are printed not glazed, but the colour reproduction is good and the models have a realistic appearance when completed. The card used is relatively thin and bracing is desirable.

The Superquick card kits are another popular series, again with a good selection of railway and other structures. These kits are made only in 00 scale. They are printed in full colour on thick card and the parts are pre-cut for ease of cutting out and folding. Clear plastic glazing material, silk screen printed with window frames is included. Construction is straightforward and results in sturdy realistic models.

The Builder Plus kits have been more recently introduced and the range, which includes 00- and N-scale models, is being steadily expanded. The models are again printed in full colour, are pre-cut and pre-creased, and include transparent silk screen printed glazing material.

This bottle kiln and workshops model in 00 scale constructed from a Novus (W & T) card kit is a small industrial unit which can be accommodated on even a very small layout, adding both scenic interest and extra goods traffic.

At the time of writing a new range, Gilmour kits, have just come on to the market, and these appear to be of similar type.

Prototype Models make a selection of card kits, printed in colour, complete with clear glazing material with printed window frames, in 2 mm, 4 mm and 7 mm scales. All the models are accurate scale replicas of actual prototype structures, mainly railway buildings. The range includes a number of models which are ideal for a branch line layout.

In addition to the British models, a variety of card kits for US and Continental prototype structures have appeared, mainly in HO scale. There are also a number of kits in varying scales, some suitable for use on model

Low relief shops built from a Hambling's Bilteezi sheet provide a neat finishing touch to Colin Woolridge's attractive N-scale layout. The houses were also built from Bilteezi kits. Note the details in the gardens.

railways, of castles and other historic buildings.

Card kits are easy to build and make a good introduction to structure modelling for the beginner. As with any kit it is important to study the parts together with any written or diagrammatic instructions before starting work. The parts should be cut out carefully, using a sharp modelling knife. The pre-cut models may still have small tabs which need cutting, rather than tearing, to avoid leaving rough edges and the risk of bending or creasing the parts. Often the number or other identifying mark is printed beside rather than on the part. To avoid any possible confusion later, mark the number lightly in pencil on the rear of each part immediately after cutting it out so that it can be definitely identified later. While this may not be important with simple models, mistakes can occur if there are more numerous parts, so this is a good habit to get into from the beginning.

Though the parts have the front surface fully coloured, the cut edges, of course, are not. When the pieces have been cut out these edges should be coloured to match the printed front surfaces using either paint or a felt-tip pen of appropriate colour. If the kit is not pre-creased the card should be scored with the knife before bending. Use a steel rule as a guide when bending to make sure the fold is straight and clean. Even with the pre-creased

Two church models in 00 scale constructed from card kits. **Below left** *A Superquick kit.* **Below right** *A Builder Plus kit.*

This realistic 4 mm scale model of Stamford Engine Shed, LNER ex-GN, was built from a Prototype Models card kit. The kits from this manufacturer are all accurate replicas of actual buildings and the range includes models in 2 mm, 4 mm and 7 mm scales. (Photograph by courtesy of Prototype Models.)

kits take care when making the bends, particularly with the smaller parts, as these can easily become distorted.

For assembly I use a quick-drying tube adhesive such as Uhu or Clear Bostik. Make sure that the parts all match up accurately before applying any glue, then use it sparingly taking care not to let any smears or blobs get on to the outer surface of the card. Some models will need extra bracing of card or stripwood inside to add strength and rigidity. If the card is not very thick it may be advisable to mount the printed walls on to thicker card before assembly. This will avoid warping, bending and buckling later and will make the models less liable to damage from handling or accidental knocks. You may want to paint the interior black or another dark colour; if so, this should be done before the roof is fitted unless access will still be possible from the bottom of the model.

If you want to fit interior details this should also be done before access becomes difficult or impossible. Even if you do not want to go to the lengths of modelling full interior detailing you may wish to add floors and dividing walls so that the viewer cannot see right through from one side of the building to the other, and so the model does not appear to be just an empty shell. These, together with just a suggestion of interior fittings, can do much to make a model look more realistic.

I have already mentioned that the Bilteezi sheets have printed and not glazed windows. While the effect is still good, particularly when the models are in the background, a more realistic appearance can undoubtedly be achieved by cutting out the windows and fitting transparent glazing material behind. On these sheets projecting brickwork is also represented by the printing and not in actual relief. An improvement is to cut this brickwork out on a second kit, mount it on thick card, touching up the edges with appropriate colour, and then glue on to the first kit as an overlay. This does require the purchase of a second kit but this is well worthwhile, especially if the model will be in the foreground on the layout. Window sills, doorsteps, and so on can be similarly treated.

There are some details which can be added to any of the kits. Doorknobs made from pinheads, guttering and downpipes from plastic strip and rod, ventilation ducts on industrial buildings from scraps of card, wood or plastic, and so on. Modelling some windows and doors in a partly open position is another realistic touch. Strips of tiles or slates, or individually applied ones, can be added, as described in the section on scratch-building, on top of the printed kit roofs giving additional relief.

Some of the printed sheets already have a weathered appearance; others will benefit from a little dirt and dust painted on, as will be discussed later. As with all model buildings, the setting is important and many details can be added to the ground around the structures.

Plastic kits The largest choice of structure models is in the form of plastic kits. As many of the manufacturers are Continental the majority of the kits are for European prototypes, though recently there has been a significant increase in the number of British prototypes available. The scales range from Z scale, for which Kibri and Märklin make a few model building kits, through to G, in which kits by HMB are designed for use with the large-scale LGB

Above *This town scene on a Fleischmann exhibition layout gives some idea of the wide range of plastic kits available in HO scale for models of European prototype structures both old and modern. Note also the realistic arrangement of the buildings on this layout.*

Below *This attractive model of a modern motor hotel, complete with rooftop café above the restaurant, is on a large Fleischmann HO-scale exhibition layout. The model was constructed from a Kibri kit.*

model railways. However, the great majority are for 00, HO and N scales.

Considering the models of British prototypes first of all, there is now a good selection available. The Airfix range in 00 scale includes a variety of railway structures. These kits are easy to assemble and form an excellent basis for further detailing and for conversions. There was also, at one time, a selection of non-railway buildings, including a windmill and a thatched cottage. These are not at present available but they may well be re-issued at a future date.

Hornby have recently brought out a range of 00-scale railway structure kits with clip-together plastic parts which are printed in full colour. These models are designed for easy construction by beginners and make up into realistic and attractive buildings especially suitable for use with the Hornby train sets.

The Danish manufacturer Heljan, in addition to Continental and American prototypes in HO and N scales, now makes a series of British railway and other building models in 00 scale which are realistic and well detailed.

In N scale Peco offer a range of railway structures, some of which are illustrated here, as well as several houses, while S & B Mouldings make kits for a selection of railway buildings.

Merit, well known for their small accessories, make a plastic kit for a typical modern signal cabin in 00 scale, and in the same scale Malvern Models have just introduced an attractive GWR halt station.

The greatest variety is in the Continental prototypes from the European manufacturers. These are mainly West German firms such as Faller, Herpa, Kibri, Pola and Vollmer, but others include Jouef (France), Heljan

This attractive signalbox in 00 scale was constructed from one of the range of pre-coloured plastic clip-together kits for model railway buildings produced by Hornby. The model includes some interior details. The trees are from Woodland Scenic kits marketed by Hammant & Morgan. (Photograph by courtesy of McLeish Associates Ltd.)

Top left and right and above left *An engine shed, goods shed and signal cabin constructed from Peco N-scale plastic kits.* (Photographs by courtesy of Peco.)

Above right *Heljan have recently introduced a range of 00-scale plastic kits for British prototype railway structures including this realistic footbridge.*

(Denmark), Lima (Italy) and Vero (East Germany). The kits are mainly in HO and N scales but include other railway scales. Though many of the models are unsuitable for use on layouts using British prototypes some, particularly the industrial structures and modern railway buildings, can be employed, if necessary with a few minor alterations. Many of the kits are remarkably well detailed and make up into excellent models. Though strictly the HO and Continental N scale models are slightly underscale for 00 and British N scale respectively the discrepancy is generally not very noticeable and the structure can be utilised.

A good selection of kits of American prototypes are also available from some of the Continental manufacturers and from American firms such as AHM, Atlas, Bachmann, Lifelike, Model Power, Revell and Tyco.

Plastic kits are generally easy to construct but, as always in modelling, care and thought will lead to the best finished model. Before starting work study the instructions and identify the parts. Remove the pieces from the sprues carefully, cutting them off with a knife or razor saw. Do not just break them off as this can cause damage at the point of attachment. Any flash or blemishes should be removed with a modelling knife, fine file and fine sandpaper. If there are any small defects these can be filled. If there are larger defects or if parts are badly formed, damaged or missing, go back to the shop where you bought the kit or write to the manufacturer direct. Many kits include complaint slips for this purpose.

This modern signal cabin was built from an 00-scale plastic kit manufactured by Merit.

This attractive 4 mm scale model GWR halt station was constructed from a plastic kit recently introduced by Malvern Models. (Photograph by courtesy of Malvern Models.)

With a simple kit where the pieces are easy to identify you can remove them all from the sprues and clean them up before assembly. With the larger, more complicated kits it is easy to confuse some of the parts. Many of them may be numbered on the pieces themselves, but others may have a number adjacent to them on the sprue and these pieces should be left in place until needed, as this will make identification easier. You may also find it easier to paint small pieces if they are left attached to the sprues, so that they can be handled and held without difficulty during painting and while they are drying. You will need to touch them up slightly when you do remove them but this is easily done. Many of the plastic kits are moulded in suitably coloured plastic so that painting is not essential. However, good painting will produce a more realistic finish. It is often easier and neater to paint some or all of the parts before assembly especially if there are small parts of one colour to be attached to a larger piece of another colour. Some parts may be inaccessible in the finished model so must be painted before or during assembly. Thus the painting sequence depends partly on the model and partly on the preferences of the builder.

The parts should be checked for a good fit by trying initially to assemble them without glue. If they do not fit together well, file or cut them to the proper shape for an accurate join. For assembly, plastic tube cement can be used but one of the liquid solvent cements such as Mek Pak is the most convenient, especially for the smaller parts. The liquid is simply painted on to the surfaces to be joined and these are then held together until firmly fixed. As the liquid is drawn by capillary action into joins, parts can be cemented conveniently by holding them together in the correct position and then drawing a brush loaded with the solvent along the join. It is important not to get either the tube cement or the solvent on to plastic surfaces which will show on the finished model as this will mark them. If this happens accidentally then wait until the cement is properly dry and hard, then file or sand off the marks, but the surface detail will also be lost. Take care not to touch the surfaces of the model if you have glue on your fingers, as this will also mark the plastic. Any cracks or gaps between parts should be filled using one of the plastic fillers available. This is another reason why it is better to paint these models even if the plastic is an appropriate colour; if you do not then you must get a perfect fit without

Graham Bailey built this market garden from his N-scale layout creating an unusual but attractive scenic feature. The greenhouses are from Faller plastic kits.

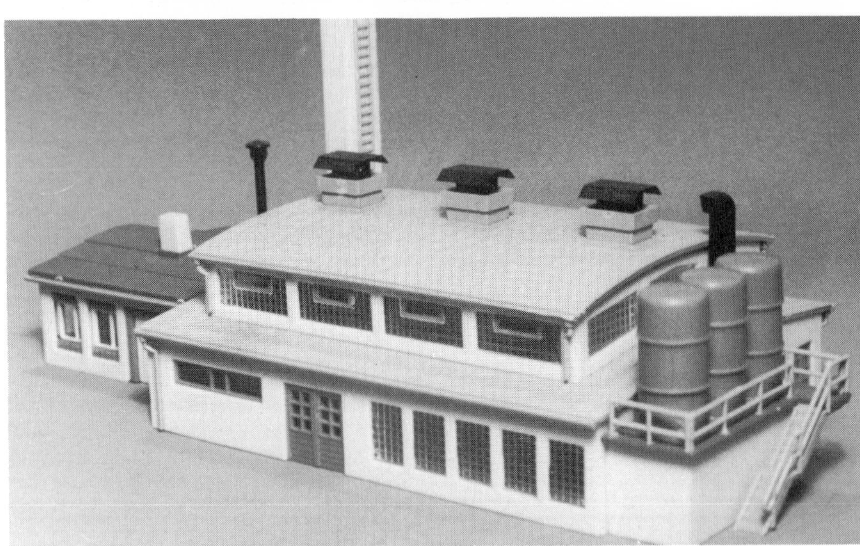

using filler, and this is not always possible. After filling, allow time for the filler to set hard then file and sand it to a smooth finish at the join.

Some of the plastic kits are very highly detailed and complete but others are more basic and will benefit from the addition of extra details as mentioned in the section on card kits.

In addition to their series of HO- and N-scale plastic kits Faller make a range of Combi kits which include embossed card parts, printed in colour, for the walls together with plastic parts and details. These kits combine the advantages of both card and plastic kits with attractive results. Lima have recently introduced a selection of British prototype building kits in 00 scale with plastic bases and roofs and pre-printed card walls. The parts slot together for easy assembly.

Scenerama produced a very neat kit for a pair of semi-detached town houses in 4 mm scale with plastic parts forming the basic structure over which brick and tilepaper were applied. Window frames, doors and other details were moulded in plastic. The completed model is very realistic but unfortunately the kit has apparently been discontinued though at the time of writing W & H Models, and perhaps other shops also, had some still in stock.

A number of structure model kits have also been made in the form of vacuum-moulded plastic. WMH Models offered a series of attractive models in 00 scale including farm buildings and ruined stone cottages. The models were ideal for both railway and military purposes but I have not seen them in the shops for some time now and I suspect they are no longer available. Houses and cottages are produced in 00 scale as vacuum-formed mouldings by Midland Model Railway Supplies and these are designed for use as low relief background models.

Wood kits In Britain manufacturers have tended to concentrate on card structure kits and there have been very few wood kits produced. Builder Plus, who make an extensive range of card kits, have recently extended the scope of their models to include two wood kits in 00 scale, a goods depot and a sawmill. These kits, which make attractive structures, include die-cut planking, stripwood of appropriate dimensions, clear glazing material and black paper to represent bitumen roofing. The goods depot is more typical of a US prototype but the sawmill is suitable for a British layout.

Marlow Models make two 4 mm scale kits of windmills. These are replicas of actual structures, Lacey Green Smock Mill and the National Trust Postmill at Pitstone Green. These are wood kits with details such as windows, millstones, etc, supplied as white metal castings. The kits can be motorised if desired.

It is in the United States, where there are many prototype structures of wooden construction, that the wood kits have been most developed. They are nearly all for HO scale though a few N-scale models are available. The structures are often of older prototypes and in many cases are exact models of particular buildings. The kits include wooden sidings, marked out or cut to size, stripwood, paper shingles, metal castings for windows, doors and other parts, and where the prototype has walls of brick or stone these are represented by brick or stonepaper, by embossed card or, in some kits, castings in dental plaster or urethane are provided. The better kits are remarkably complete even to posters and signs for the walls, and the instructions are often very detailed, even including advice on weathering and providing a proper scenic setting. In some kits there are dozens, even hundreds, of white metal castings for detailing purposes and full interior detailing may be provided, as in the Fine Scale Miniatures Rail Car Shed kit illustrated.

As some experience in modelling is desirable these American kits are not really intended for the beginner but with time, care and some skill, models of exhibition standard can be built from them. Not surprisingly, these kits tend to cost more than the mass-produced card or plastic kits and the larger and more complex ones are quite expensive. However, they do provide many enjoyable hours of construction and a fine model afterwards. These 'craftsman' wood kits are available in limited numbers in Britain at specialist shops such as Victors of Islington.

While the British wood kits are less complicated than many of the US models, construction is more difficult than for card and plastic kits, and a little previous modelling experience will be helpful. It is important to read the instructions or study the diagrams carefully before starting work and to identify

Top left *A realistic girder bridge constructed from a Vollmer plastic kit carries an electrified branch over the main line on this N-scale German layout, based on a prototype. Note how the bridge supporting walls are set into the scenery without any unsightly gaps or cracks.*

Centre left and left *There are many interesting industrial structures available as plastic kits from Continental manufacturers. These pictures show two examples in N scale. A modern chemical factory from the Vollmer range and a timber plant from Pola.*

Above left and right *Marlow Models have recently introduced two kits for 4 mm scale windmills which are models of actual prototype structures—Lacey Green Smock Mill and Pitstone Postmill. The kits are wood with cast metal parts such as windows and millstones.* (Photographs by Angy Jackman.)

Below *Wood craftsman kits are popular in the United States. This superb HO-scale coal dock was constructed by C. Emmerson from a Fine Scale Miniatures kit.* (Photograph by courtesy of Fine Scale Miniatures.)

Above far right *The roof has been removed from this HO-scale rail car shed built from a Fine Scale Miniatures kit to show the incredibly detailed interior. Everything shown, with the exception of the human figures, is included in this remarkably complete kit.* (Photograph by courtesy of Fine Scale Miniatures.)

correctly the materials to be used for each part. It is easy to use the wrong stripwood, for example, so that later you find you have not sufficient of a particular size. In the Builder Plus kits many identical parts must be cut and assembled and care is required to do this accurately. This is important because errors here will spoil the appearance of the completed building. Tube adhesive such as Uhu or Bostik, or balsa cement can be used for assembly. Allow sufficient time for the cement to harden before trying to proceed with construction as many of the separate items are rather fragile until fitted together and if the glue has not set firmly these units may distort while you are fixing them in place. The models can be painted or alternatively stained to represent weathered, unpainted wood. The modeller with a little experience, particularly if he has done some aero-modelling in which the construction work is rather similar, will find that he can build successfully from these kits and that the resulting models are realistic wooden structures. The kits are also a good introduction to this type of work for those who would like to go on to scratch-building models of wooden prototypes.

Metal kits In Britain these are restricted to cast metal kits and the cost and weight of this material limits the choice to small structures such as lineside huts. Mike's Models offer cast metal kits in 4 mm scale for a GWR pagoda halt station building, a Victorian cast iron 'gents' and a GWR corrugated iron lamp hut. Roxey Mouldings make 4 mm scale kits for a Southern Railway platelayers' hut and a tool hut and the Dart Castings range, also 00-scale, includes a GWR lineside hut. W & H Models make a 4 mm scale 'gents' white metal kit. In N scale Fleetline Models make lineside huts and girder and plate girder railway bridges.

Assembly of these small cast metal kits is straightforward. The castings should be cleaned up with a fine file to remove any flash and to ensure a good fit of the parts. The pieces can then be assembled using a tube cement such as Bostik, an epoxy adhesive or a cyanoacrylate adhesive. After washing the model with warm water and a little detergent to remove any dirt and grease it can be painted. For priming I find Duplicolor Grey Primer, supplied in aerosol cans for car touching-up work, convenient, followed by Humbrol or other model paint for the final coats.

In the United States another type of metal kit is available from Suydam. These HO-scale models, mainly of mines and other industrial structures, are made from metal with a corrugated surface covering representing corrugated iron. Assembly requires soldering.

Plaster kits A very effective method of reproducing brick and stone walls is to model a handmade original, make a mould from it and then cast the parts in plaster. These walls are then glued together to form the building and are painted as required. Ossett Mouldings produced a very useful range of castings of this type, including the roof tiling used on the factory model shown on page 33, using plaster with a reinforcing backing of cloth. This firm also made a series of structure kits including lineside huts and a half-timbered pub in this material. Unfortunately I think they must have been discontinued as I have not been able to

With the Linka system the modeller uses the moulds provided to cast parts which can then be used to make up a wide variety of 00-scale model buildings. Two examples, a farm and a castle, are shown in these pictures. (Photographs by courtesy of Thomas Salter Ltd.)

The main roof is made from roofing tiles mouldings from the Ossett range of plastic castings. The ventilator duct was assembled from stripwood with thin strips of plastic card around it (see also page 39).

find any in the shops recently. Some of the US manufacturers, as I have already mentioned, include castings in dental plaster in their 'craftsman' type wooden kits, where stonework is needed.

Thomas Salter have taken a different approach in their new and justifiably popular Linka system. In these sets the modeller is provided with a wide range of moulds for brick and stonework, logs and lapboard, including window openings, doorways and so on, together with Linkalite casting compound. Windows of various types printed on clear glazing material are available and guttering, drainpipes and sheets of signs are also provided for detailing purposes. The parts are supplied as kits of various selections, for example, brickwork or stonework, but are also available separately. Plans, giving full details of the parts needed and how they must be assembled, are produced for a range of 00-scale structures of interest to the railway and military modeller but, of course, the scope for constructing models of the builder's own choice or design is almost limitless.

The system is easy to use. The mould required is first prepared by rinsing it with a little washing-up liquid in warm water. The Linkalite Moulding Compound is gently mixed with water using the measures provided and is then poured into the mould cavities, taking care to push it well into all the corners. The mould is tapped to remove any air bubbles and, as the mixture begins to set, a straight edge is drawn across the surface of the mould to scrape off any excess mixture. After about half an hour the casting is removed by flexing the mould and easing the rubber away. It is then left to dry for 24 hours at room temperature or for four to eight hours in an airing cupboard.

The castings interlock for assembly and they are fixed together with a little of the adhesive provided. Windows, cut from the printed glazing material supplied, are glued in place behind the window openings. Basic paints are provided in the sets but poster paints, ordinary household emulsions or Humbrol enamels can also be employed for colouring.

There is a special thatch-making kit with brushes and a special slow setting Linkalite compound so that the surface can be textured to represent this type of roofing.

Because the moulds can be re-used as often as the modeller wishes and additional moulding compound, adhesive and other items can be purchased separately, the system has great scope and flexibility for the scratch-builder as well as the kit modeller.

Kit conversion

I have already mentioned the possibility of adding extra details to make kit structures more interesting and realistic. From this the modeller may well progress to kit conversion in which the kit is modified so that the finished model has a different appearance. There are several possible advantages in this. It can provide variety and individuality in your structures, and can make kit buildings more suitable for the type of scene you are modelling or for the location in which your layout is supposed to be set. It also enables you to construct more easily, more quickly and perhaps, more successfully than by scratch-building, models of buildings for which no kits are produced. It will, generally however, be more expensive than building entirely from scratch.

Obviously your own interests and the amount of time you can devote to modelling will influence how you choose to model structures. If you are keenest on operation you may be happy to use only basic kit-built structures, perhaps the quickly assembled clip-together Hornby kits for 00 scale, or even, if you are working in N scale, the ready built models made by Grafar. If your interests are more general and include construction as well as operation you may want to convert kits so that you can enjoy more interesting structure modelling and also give your layout some individuality. Alternatively you might particularly like building construction and find that this becomes a main interest in the hobby. In this case you may want to spend most of your time making highly detailed structure models from scratch while keeping other aspects of your layout relatively simple. Indeed, one of the nice things about railway modelling is the wide choice it offers. While I do enjoy scratch-building, my free time is limited and this is one reason why I convert kits. However, I also like the challenge which this type of modelling presents.

The scope of kit conversion is very wide,

Above left *The Airfix 00-scale signalbox plastic kit is also useful as a starting point for conversion work. This picture shows the basic kit assembled according to the manufacturer's instructions.*

Left *A view of a 4 mm scale gantry signal cabin. The cabin itself was constructed from parts of an Airfix signalbox kit while the supporting gantry was made up from Plastruct girdering. The stairs from two kits were used and the additional handrails required for the stairs and around the cabin were cut from thin plastic card.*

Right *This small signalbox for a 4 mm scale narrow-gauge line was largely scratch-built from plastic card but parts from the Airfix signalbox kit were used for convenience. Kit parts used included cut down sides and stairs.*

Below right *Terry Jenkins built this 00-scale factory using Hambling's Bilteezi dairy/small factory card kits. The crane is from an Airfix military vehicle plastic kit.*

Bottom *Keith Gowen constructed the station buildings for the terminus on his TT-scale branch line from Hambling's Bilteezi Stone Forge card kits. The platform canopy is a scratch-built addition.*

ranging from minor alterations in appearance, for example, in modifying a Continental structure to make it look more typical of a British building, to using a few kit parts in a model where so much is fabricated from other materials that the structure could more accurately be considered as scratch-built. This latter situation is not as extravagant as it may at first seem. Many plastic kits are relatively inexpensive but contain well detailed parts which cannot be obtained as separate items. To make up these parts from scratch may be difficult and time consuming and, for the inexperienced modeller, the final result will probably not be as good as the kit parts. Thus it may be worth the cost of the kit to obtain the parts you want; the rest of the kit can be kept and may well provide parts for further conversions in the future. The two signalbox models illustrated here utilise the more-difficult-to-fabricate parts such as sides, with windows, and the steps, from Airfix Signal Cabin kits resulting in a considerable saving in time and work compared to scratch-building. Do take care when converting or using kit parts that the kit or components are suitable for the model you are attempting to make and that the alterations will not involve more work than building from scratch. It can be rather easy to get so carried away with the idea of converting

Two views of an interesting conversion from an 00-scale Super-quick low relief card kit. The modeller has used parts from a second kit to alter the low relief models to full-depth structures. Note the painters on the centre roof and the bird on the higher roofs.

that it can become an end of its own rather than a means to an end. Remember that the idea is to enable you to build a model more easily and quickly, and perhaps with a better result, than if you were to try to build it from scratch.

The card kits are easy to convert and some examples are shown in this book. Many others have been described in the model railway magazines over the years. R.G. Vacy-Ash, the designer of the Hambling's Bilteezi sheets, has built several attractive models converted from these kits and, in fact, some of the kits have been designed to permit construction in different forms. Another well-known modeller, the Rev Edward Beal, has also made a number of interesting models by converting these kits.

However, the plastic kits offer the greatest possibilities for the kit converter and the scope is almost unlimited. I made a point of collecting all the catalogues issued by the structure kit manufacturers so that I can check on just what is available. Just browsing through these will often give me an idea for a conversion. Familiarity with the kits on the market also means that when I see a prototype structure I like I may recall a kit which would be a suitable basis for conversion into a model of this building or which might provide suitable parts for an otherwise scratch-built model.

Whenever you carry out any kit construction or conversion always save any left-over parts. In time you will build up a very useful selection which you can utilise for further projects. As these parts accumulate it is worth separating them into different items such as doors, windows, stairway parts, chimneys, piping, handrails, sections of brick, stone or wood planking, and so on. Store the different lots in labelled boxes or small drawers so that you can quickly check through to see just what you have and so that you can find any particular item without delay. I also keep the instruction sheet from any kit I assemble in a file so that I can refer to it again. Checking through these can also be helpful in finding suitable parts for conversions as most of these sheets include diagrams showing all the kit parts.

A common form of conversion is the combination of two or more identical kits to form a larger structure. This is usually fairly straightforward and, indeed, some kits are designed to permit this as an alternative to the single kit form. Several of the engine shed kits, both card and plastic, come into this category. However, others particularly for factories, warehouses, goods sheds and mine buildings can often be assembled without difficulty with two or more kits combined.

For the more complex conversions quite drastic alterations may be required with extensive cutting and fitting of the parts. These models must be carefully planned and the parts accurately marked and cut if we are to avoid mistakes which may be difficult to rectify. If pieces are wrongly cut it may even be necessary to buy an extra kit to replace the parts and this can be annoying and expensive! Walls, roofs and bases are usually of fairly thick

A medium-sized engine shed constructed in N scale by combining four Peco engine shed kits. The kit is designed to allow any number of units to be fitted together to form a suitable-sized shed. (Photograph by courtesy of Peco.)

plastic and this is most easily cut with a razor saw. Use a file and sandpaper for cleaning up the cut edges and to achieve a perfect fit. If the rear wall of a structure will not be visible when the model is placed on the layout the part or parts making up this wall can be replaced by thick card if desired and the kit wall used elsewhere in the conversion. In this way I was able to construct the small factory (shown in some of the photographs) from a single Airfix engine shed kit even though the factory is twice as long as the kit structure.

When carrying out a conversion you may need to fill in some window or door openings. There may be left over parts from the kit, or from previous conversions, which can be used to fill these gaps or you may need to employ plastic card, either plain material scribed to match, or embossed brick or stone sheet. Any gaps or cracks should be filled, then filed and sanded smooth in the usual way. Joins between parts, for example, in the middle of a wall, can often be concealed by appropriately placed drainpipes, notices, posters, ventilation ducts, piping, lean-to buildings, even planks of wood leaning against the wall.

If in a conversion the cut edge of a section of stone course or brick wall is visible at a corner of the building, a fine file or model knife should be used to carry the grooves representing the mortar between the brick or stone courses around the corner to give a more realistic

A neat N-scale overbridge using Peco moulded plastic girder bridge sides. The stonework is embossed plastic card. Longer bridges can be constructed by employing more than one pair of sides. (Photograph by courtesy of Peco.)

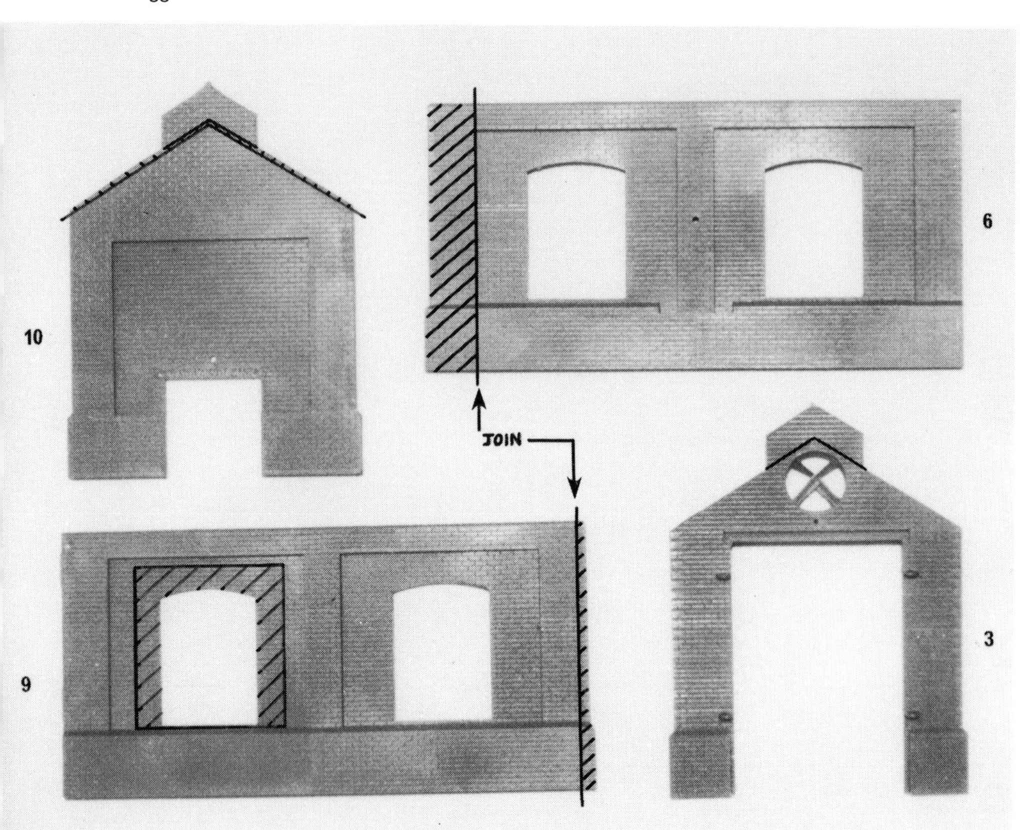
10
6
JOIN
9
3

The Airfix 00-scale engine shed plastic kit is an excellent basis for conversion work and these pictures illustrate the construction of a small lineside factory using parts from this kit. **Left** *Parts from the kit showing how they are modified. Cuts were made with a razor saw. Numbers refer to the kit part numbers. Parts 6 and 9 are joined to form the front wall of the factory.* **Below left** *Front, rear and ends assembled and windows fitted. As the rear of the model will not be visible on the layout, plain card was used for this wall. Alternatively parts from a second kit could be employed to model this wall more fully.* **Above** *A loading platform cut from wood together with doors and a canopy made from balsa wood have been added. The lean-to at the right-hand end was constructed from thick card covered with corrugated copper sheet. The additional roof supports are thick card.* **Below** *The completed model with roof added. See also photograph on page 33.*

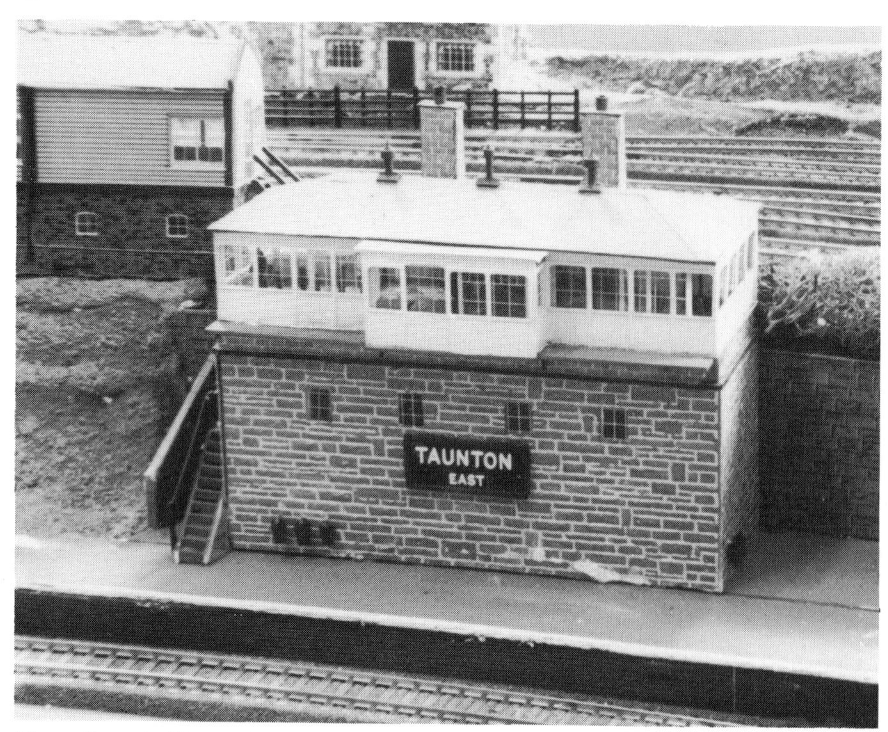

Above *Terry Jenkins used parts from Airfix signal box kits together with a scratch-built base for this large signalbox on the Bournemouth & Isle of Purbeck MRC 4 mm scale layout.*

Below *Graham Bailey used Pola station roof kits with additional parts scratch-built from card for the large station on his N-scale modern layout. The fire station in the foreground was constructed from a Hambling's Bilteezi card kit.*

appearance. Additional parts needed for a conversion, if not to be found in the scrap parts box, can be modelled from plastic card, wood, card or other materials as in scratch-building.

When carrying out conversion work there is no need for the modeller to restrict himself to a single kit or to two or more identical kits. Different kits can be combined with advantage giving great scope for variety, a form of modelling sometimes known as 'cross kitting'. Some models may utilise parts from quite a number of different kits. It all depends on what parts appear most suitable and on the contents of your spare parts box. It is also possible, with a little care, successfully to combine kits of different materials, for example, card and plastic, making the scope even greater. In such cases the plastic parts should be painted, and overall weathering is useful to tone down any differences in surface texture and in colour between the painted plastic and printed card parts. Balsa or hardwood is useful for constructing wooden additions such as lean-to sheds and outbuildings.

One of the advantages of kit conversion is that by building a variety of structures all based on one or two kits we can create a similarity of style and construction material which will give unity and harmony to the scene, enhancing the realism and atmosphere. Railway buildings in a particular area, for example, often show this sort of similarity due to standardisation of architectural style, construction materials and the design of small fittings and details by the railway company concerned.

As the projects become more complex and advanced the work tends to merge into scratch-building and when the modeller comes across a structure which cannot be conveniently converted from any available kit he should find no difficulty in tackling its construction from scratch.

Kit conversion has now outgrown the somewhat derogatory 'kit bashing' title it was once given and is a valuable form of structure modelling. It provides interest and variety without the commitment in time and work required for scratch-building and, best of all, it can be great fun!

Working models

Some modellers dislike structure models which have moving parts, regarding them as gimmicky. Perhaps this follows from the manufacture of toy train gadgetry such as exploding boxcars, head-bobbing giraffes and so on, leading the scale modeller to feel that all working structures and accessories are out of place on a scale layout. However, the kits available are generally well detailed and realistic models which are entirely suitable for use on a scale model railway. The extra movement and interest which these working models can add to the scene are of benefit, particularly on a small layout where the train-operating potential may be rather limited. One of the most popular subjects is the windmill and a variety of types are available in both HO and N scales from Faller and Pola, and in HO scale from Vero. One of the HO-scale Faller kits is for a windmill complete with a waterwheel as well. These models are all of Continental prototypes and will require modifications to make them more typical of British mills. However, the Marlow Models 4 mm scale wooden windmill kits can be motorised by the modeller if desired and these are replicas of actual British windmills. Another attractive choice is a watermill with kits in HO and N scale by Faller and Pola. The Faller HO model is remarkable in that the wheel is driven round by real water which is circulated by means of a small pump. This pump can also be employed to provide moving water for model fountains and waterfalls. Brawa also make a pump of this type. The Faller range also includes sawmills in HO and N scales with waterwheels. As with the windmill kits the prototypes are typically European and modification is needed for a British layout.

The windmills and watermills are appropriate for a rural setting but there are also kits for working models suitable for industrial areas. Vollmer make a working conveyor-belt in HO scale which can be used in conjunction with a loading platform and a warehouse and this will add extra activity to a goods depot or industrial scene. Faller also offer a working conveyor-belt in this scale which can be combined with a dumping tip and storage hopper as part of an interesting gravel works complex. A very effective item from Brawa is an HO-scale working model of an aerial ropeway of the type used to carry ore, rock, coal and so on from a mine or quarry to a processing plant. This firm also uses a similar mechanism for models of a cable railway in HO and N scales and a ski-lift in HO scale. These latter two are more suited to layouts based on Continental prototypes but the mineral ropeway is ideal for British or European model railways.

Container terminals are now part of the

This HO-scale Pola windmill is fitted with a small electric motor to make the sails rotate. The model adds movement as well as scenic interest on this small 009 layout owned by the Poole & District MRS. Note the many small details which make the scene appear larger than it really is.

Above left *An interesting 4 mm scale model of the beam pump at Wheal Busy built by Steve Dewhirst. The building was constructed from card which was painted with shellac and then coated with a thin layer of Polyfilla. When dry this was smoothed over and the stonework was scribed into it. Painting was with poster colours. The chimney is made from plastic card with computer punchings glued on to simulate bricks. The working parts for the beam engine were fabricated from plastic card.*

Above right *Another interesting working model is this cable car system manufactured by Eheim and seen here on a Continental layout built by Terry Jenkins. Models are available in both HO and N scales.*

British railway scene and Faller produce a working model in HO scale which is suitable for a large or moderate-sized goods depot on a modern image layout. If your model railway serves a dock you might like to include one of the impressive Wiad HO scale dockside cranes. Powered by four motors the crane can move along on rails on the dockside, or along on its own bridge track, can rotate and can lift a load, all by remote control.

Lifting bridges are not uncommon on full-size railways and they make interesting models. Working versions of a rolling lift bridge were available in N and HO scales from Pola; the HO-scale model was later marketed by Hornby. However, I am not certain about the present availability of these two models.

There is, of course, no reason why the modeller should not convert the working model kits in the same way as ordinary structure kits. Alternatively the motors and other mechanism parts can be utilised for scratch-built models, or the modeller can buy suitable motors as separate items and make up the remainder of the parts needed from metal or plastic. An example of an interesting and authentic 00-scale working model of a Cornish tin mine beam pump and winding engine scratch-built by Steve Dewhirst is illustrated here. Steve used plastic card to make the working parts and the pump is driven by a slow-speed mains synchronous motor. The mine is the central feature of a small 009 model railway layout and below baseboard level Steve has included part of the network of passages and caverns which would make up the underground workings, creating a most unusual and intriguing model.

Whether or not to include working model structures on a model railway layout is obviously a matter of personal choice but I feel that these models do warrant serious consideration particularly on a small layout where any extra movement and activity which can be provided will add to the interest. They are also popular with visitors to model railway shows and therefore can be fitted on to exhibition layouts to advantage.

Scratch-building

The construction of a model from basic materials is often known as scratch-building and it offers the greatest choice of subject and materials, though does, of course, involve more work, both in actual construction and in the preparation needed beforehand. This preliminary work involves choosing the subject and acquiring the necessary data, obtaining or drawing up plans, selecting and assembling the various materials. Once all this is done you can plan out your order of construction and begin the actual modelling. If you are working from a fully detailed plan you may find it convenient to trace from it a simplified version showing only the basic dimensions of the walls and the sizes and positions of the window, door and other openings. You can then work from this when constructing the basic shell without being confused by all the additional details which are not important at this stage. This will make the job easier and quicker with less chance of making errors.

Various materials can be employed for the basic structure. The surface finish may be modelled by working on the outer surface of this basic shell or may be in the form of an overlay applied to it. Most modellers use card, wood (balsa, hardwood or ply), or plastic card but other materials such as plaster or expanded polystyrene can be employed just as successfully. If card is used we have a choice of two methods. The whole building can be drawn in opened-out form on the card, with or without the roof, as in simple cut-out card models. After cutting out the walls in one piece, the door and window openings are also cut out. The corners are then scored or cut part way through with a knife and are bent using a metal straight-edge held behind to act as a guide so that the corners are folded sharply and accurately. The basic form is then bent to shape with the two ends brought together to form the fourth corner. Gummed paper tape can be applied to hold the ends at this corner and pieces of stripwood added inside each corner will give the structure strength and

Above, above right and right *Stages in construction of the canal coal staithe. The concrete base was built up from wood. The deck, cut from balsa wood sheet, and the girdering, from Plastruct, have been added. The loading chute was built up from plastic card. The steps are from an Airfix footbridge kit with Slater's handrail posts and rails of Microrod.*

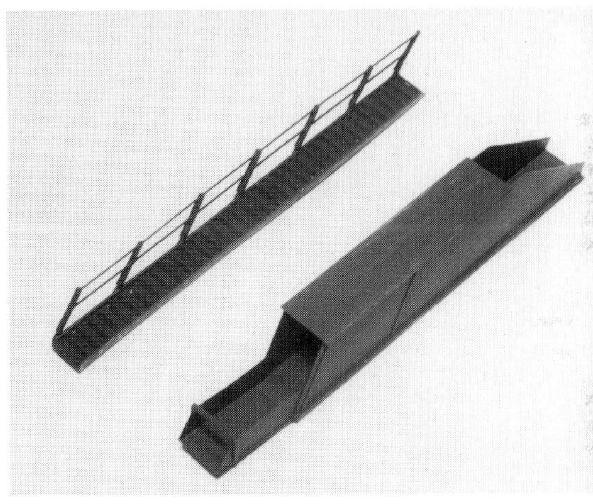

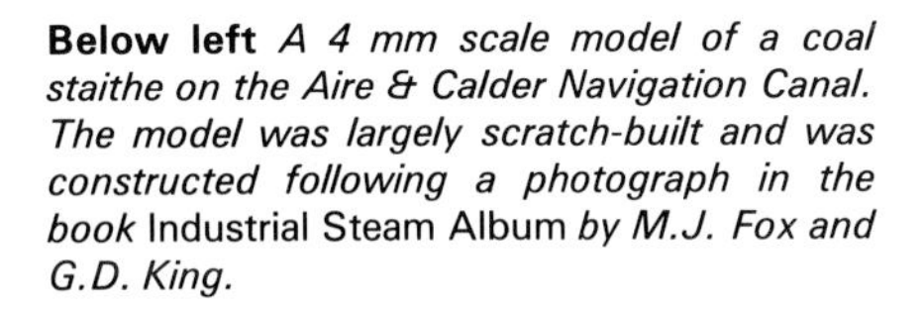

Below left *A 4 mm scale model of a coal staithe on the Aire & Calder Navigation Canal. The model was largely scratch-built and was constructed following a photograph in the book* Industrial Steam Album *by M.J. Fox and G.D. King.*

rigidity. A further inner wall, also of card, can be fitted inside each wall. In these inner walls the window and door openings are also cut out but slightly smaller than the openings in the outer walls to form the window and door frames. With these inner walls glued in place the structure will be quite sturdy. If you plan to use brick or stonepaper on the walls this should be applied before the inner walls are fitted.

Alternatively the walls can be cut out separately from card, wood or plastic card. Either the corners must be bevelled to fit, or you must allow for two of the walls to fit inside the others, for example, the ends between the front and back, and subtract the thickness of the front and back from the width of the end walls. With this method they can either be assembled immediately after cutting out to form a basic structure similar to the folded card type, or each wall can be fully modelled before being assembled with the others. This latter method can be very convenient, especially if there are additional facings and fittings or signs and lettering to be applied, as such work can then be carried out with the walls laid flat on the workbench. If card is used, stripwood bracing will again be desirable in the corners but with wood it may not be required. When working with plastic card I usually fit triangular pieces of scrap plastic into the corners to hold them square and to strengthen the structure generally. Interior walls and floors are best added after the windows have been fitted. The choice of material for the basic shell is not important but it is essential that the structure is accurate in dimensions and squareness (unless deliberate distortion is to be introduced to model an old prototype), and sturdy so that it will not become warped or twisted later.

An example of an unconventional material which has been employed recently is expanded polystyrene. This packing material is light and strong and is convenient for modelling the basic structure of buildings. It is especially

L N E R

popular for ruined buildings on military dioramas. The plastic is easily cut with a knife, saw or, best of all, a hot wire cutter. The construction of such a device has been described by Dave Rowe in an article in the August 1979 issue of *Model Railways* magazine. The surface of the expanded polystyrene can be scribed to represent stonework but the finish is rather coarse and a better effect is achieved by covering the plastic with Polyfilla, Das or Artex. To assemble a structure most universal adhesives are satisfactory but ordinary polystyrene cements must not be used as they will dissolve the expanded plastic.

There are various surface finishes we can choose and these can be modelled in a number of different ways. The choice is up to the individual modeller for the most part and I would recommend that the reader try out different materials and techniques before deciding on which are selected. In the following sections I will endeavour to cover the main ones in use. All give good results if used with care.

The traditional method for modelling brickwork is to use brickpaper and this is still a very satisfactory system. Suitable papers, printed in full colour, are available from various manufacturers. The colouring is generally good and in some cases the brickwork is represented with a realistic weathered appearance. The paper is glued on to the basic structure. When applying the paper to card I often use photomount spray but other adhesives are equally suitable. If plastic card is employed for the basic form, the paper can be applied easily by placing it on the plastic and then painting solvent adhesive liberally on to it. The solvent soaks through the paper and bonds it to the plastic. I apply the paper to each wall separately allowing for an overlap of about $\frac{1}{4}$ in around the corners for the front and back walls. The paper is then fixed on to the end walls and covers this overlap. This method strengthens the corners and avoids the risk of the paper peeling away from the corners as it might if the paper on all the walls goes up to but not around the corners. Use a modelling knife and cut diagonally across the window openings; fold the four flaps thus formed back and glue them to the inside of the walls. In this way the edge of the openings are covered with the brickpaper giving a neat and realistic appearance. Treat the door openings in a similar way.

Stonepapers are employed in exactly the same way as are the brickpapers and also give

Top left *Most of this large N-scale factory complex was scratch-built from 1 mm thick card by Graham Bailey. Brickwork is represented by a covering of Builder Plus brickpaper. The structures at the right-hand end were built from Hambling's Bilteezi sheets.*

Left *An unusual but realistic and interesting model is this derelict factory modelled in N scale by Graham Bailey. The walls are 1 mm thick card covered with Builder Plus brickpaper; beams and rafters are balsa stripwood.*

Below left *Bridges on the 'Eight Oaks' N-scale layout built by Bob Jones. The bridge in the foreground was constructed from stripwood while the stone structure behind is of wooden construction with a covering of stonepaper.*

Below *Terry Jenkins scratch-built this small goods shed in 00 scale using Faller embossed card of stone wall pattern for the walls.*

an attractive finish when applied carefully. Faller make a selection of brick and stone facings which are printed in full colour on card and are embossed to give a more realistic surface texture. These are designed for HO scale but are also suitable for 00. The sheets are applied in a similar manner to brick and stonepapers except that their greater thickness makes it advisable to cut out the window and door openings and not to fold flaps back.

Another popular method now is the use of embossed plastic card for brick and stonework. This material is thin so must be applied as a facing, usually on to a shell made up from thicker plastic card. It can be fixed on the plain walls either before or after they are assembled. Care must be taken to make a square cut along the bottom edge before fitting the facing on so that the brick or stone courses will be parallel to the lower edge of the walls. This cut should be along one of the mortar lines so that the courses on each wall will align properly at the corners. Ideally the corners should be bevelled so that the courses appear to go round the corners. Alternatively, a fine file or modelling knife can be used to make grooves in the edge of the facing piece when a butt joint is used, to match up with the grooves on the adjacent piece. The window and door openings are cut out neatly and if necessary filed true. A fine file or knife is also used here to extend the courses on to the cut edge of the apertures giving the impression of a solid brick or stone wall. The embossed plastic must be painted an appropriate colour depending on the type of brick or stone you wish to represent. A good effect of pointing can then be achieved by applying a thin cream of Polyfilla or Artex over the wall and rubbing most of it gently off. After it has dried further a second rub over will remove any filler which is not in the grooves. The material remaining in the courses gives a realistic representation of the mortar.

A very effective but more time consuming method is to scribe the brick or stonework in the card of the basic structure. This is the technique employed for some of the superb Pendon models. The walls are International Pasteboard and are scribed with a blunt point following the prototype brick or stonework as exactly as possible. An overall coat of paint of mortar colour is applied and then the bricks or stones are touched in individually, varying the colours slightly, giving a very realistic texture and colour.

An alternative, and even more time consuming, method is the application of individual bricks or stones. These are cut from paper, thin card or thin plastic card. A very useful source of rectangles of card of approximately the right size for 00-scale bricks is the punchings from computer cards and if you can obtain some of these you can save yourself a great deal of time and effort by not having to cut out your bricks. The bricks or stones are then positioned one by one on adhesive which has been coated over the basic wall surfaces. The easiest way to do this is to pick the bricks and stones up with the point of a needle. Later the whole is painted as described above for the scribed walls.

A different technique is to use household

Terry Jenkins again used Kos fire cement for the coaling stage and the base of the water tower in this model of the engine servicing facilities at Swanage on the Bournemouth & Isle of Purbeck MRC layout.

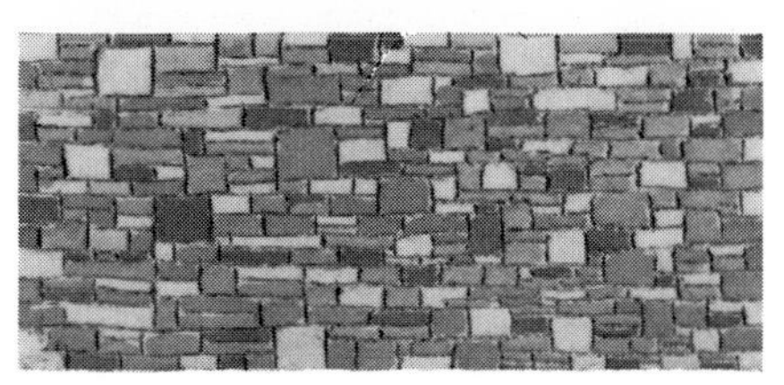

Coursed stonework of two different types modelled with Peco Texture Modelling Compound. Variation in the colour of the stones in painting adds to the effect. (Photograph by courtesy of Peco.)

filler such as Polyfilla or Tapwata applied as a coating over a shell of thick card or balsa wood. The brick or stone courses are then scribed into the filler either while it is still soft or after it has dried and hardened. I have used this method effectively for stonework and see no reason why it should not also be satisfactory for brick walls, though the latter will be more work to produce.

The modelling clay Das and fire cements such as Kos can be used in a similar way over wood or card shells. An application of PVA adhesive before the Das or Kos is spread on will make sure that the coating of clay or cement will not come away from the shell as it dries. These materials are scribed before they set. This should be done with a sharp modelling knife taking care to leave only a groove and not to raise a ridge at either side of the groove. Such ridges are unsightly and unrealistic and make it obvious that the material has been scribed, thus spoiling the illusion we are trying to create of a wall made up of separate bricks or stones. When dry the model is painted appropriately using model paints.

Peco Texture Modelling Compound is very useful for modelling brick and stonework. The material is spread over a wood or card shell which has been built up in the usual way and while still moist is scribed to represent the brick or stone walling. The compound remains workable indefinitely provided it is kept moist, and by laying a damp cloth over partially completed work the modeller can leave it and return to it when convenient. The material dries to a natural stone colour but can be painted to give other colours. An inexpensive method is to use household emulsion with powder poster colours mixed in as necessary to give the required shades. Alternatively ordinary model paints can be employed.

I have already described the Linka system in the section on kits and kit construction but, of course the sections of brick and stonework which can be made with the Linka moulds can be used just as successfully for scratch-built models. Modellers can also take the process

A Welsh farmhouse beautifully modelled in 4 mm scale by Dave Rowe using Peco Texture Modelling Compound. This model can be seen at the Peco Modelrama exhibition in Beer, Devon. (Photograph by courtesy of Peco.)

further and make their own moulds. This involves the construction of a master and the making of a mould from it. This is then used to cast as many copies as required. Various materials can be used for the master and for the mould. The master, for example, can be wood or dental plaster carved to represent stonework, or can be made from Das scribed to produce a similar result. The mould itself can be latex, white silicone rubber, or Meltamould remeltable rubber made by Turner Research Ltd of Leeds. This last is available from many toyshops. The final castings can be made from Linkalite or one of the other commercially produced casting powders or from dental plaster, available from Boots chemists.

Trevor Hughes, in addition to casting stonework from his own moulds using techniques similar to those mentioned above, has devised an ingenious and very effective method for modelling stone-built cottages and other structures. He casts a simple slab of plaster about $\frac{3}{8}$ in thick. This is then cut up into individual blocks of stone and these are used to build up the structure block by block giving a very realistic appearance. The process was described fully in the May 1979 issue of *Airfix Magazine.*

Another method of modelling brick and stone walls for model building is by detailing balsa wood with a wood-burning pen or Pyrogravure. The tool is used to make the grooves between the stones or bricks by burning them into the surface of the wood. A metal rule is used to guide the burning pen. I have used this method very satisfactorily for stonework. Brickwork can also be modelled successfully but the tip of my woodburning tool is not really quite fine enough for this. This instrument is also ideal for modelling wood planking. The narrow-gauge engine and carriage shed illustrated here has a wooden extension which was made by this method. The walls are balsa with the grain running vertically. The wood-burning pen was used to make the grooves between the planks and also to create the appearance of splits, cracks and knots in the planking. This was easily and quickly carried out. The pen does darken the wood where the burning takes place so painting is necessary.

In the United States an excellent selection of stripwood is available enabling modellers to build up models of wooden prototype structures almost as board by board replicas of the originals. This method is very time consuming but the results can be superb.

Plaster and other textured finishes for walls of buildings can be modelled by coating the basic walls with PVA adhesive and sprinkling on fine sand or other material. When dry the walls can be painted. Many industrial buildings are of corrugated iron construction and this can be modelled with corrugated copper (Slater) or aluminium (Campbell Scale Models) sheet in 00 and HO scales. For the best appearance cut the model corrugated iron into scale-size sheets and apply these individually to the basic shell. Weathering and streaks of rust will give the finishing touches after painting.

When the walls have been modelled the windows can be added. The window frames are usually cut from card or plastic card and can be painted before fixing in place. Clear plastic glazing material represents the glass conveniently. The glazing bars can be painted or scribed on the clear plastic. If scribed, the bars can be coloured by smearing on a little paint and then rubbing it off; the little which remains in the scribed grooves will colour them. A convenient alternative is the use of 'Downesglaze' a clear plastic with silk screen printed frames and glazing bars. This was designed by expert structure modeller, Allan Downes, and gives a realistic appearance with a minimum of effort for the modeller.

If desired, the glazing bars can be incorporated when cutting out the window frames. This is tricky and time consuming and must be done neatly, but can be very effective. Another popular method is to use the neat and ingenious Slater grid system. This manufacturer produces fine plastic card strip, notched at intervals. Lengths of this strip can be fitted together by the notches to produce a grid of the size required for the window. A variety of notch spacings allows the modeller to select the strip needed for the pane sizes he wants. The grid system is easy to use and results in very neat windows.

An alternative to plastic glazing which is preferred by some of the experts is thin glass such as microscope cover slips which are used to cover specimens on slides before they are placed under the microscope. This thin glass is easily snapped to size after scoring and is ideal for modelling windows. One advantage is that it does not become warped, as can occur with plastic.

Bay windows are best modelled as separate units which are then added to the basic structure after they are complete. Construction can be from card or plastic card with clear plastic glazing following the usual methods of construction employed for the main structure.

Doors are modelled in a similar way to windows with the frame and then the door itself fitted behind. A realistic touch is to model some of the windows and perhaps one of the doors of a building in the open position. This

Above *For this 1:64 scale model of the bridge below Tan-Y-Bwlch station on the Ffestiniog Railway, Trevor Hughes cast the abutments in situ from plaster and then scribed them with a sharp needle to represent the stonework. The main bridge girders were cast in epoxy resin in a rubber mould and the handrails are expanded metal.*

Below *Beautifully modelled stone cottage and outbuildings from a prototype at Blaenau Ffestiniog. The model was constructed by Trevor Hughes for a 1:64 scale narrow-gauge model railway layout and the walls were built up from separate blocks cut from cast plaster to represent the stone blocks of the real structure.*

Two views of a scratch-built engine and carriage shed for a 4 mm scale narrow-gauge railway layout. The stone buildings were modelled with walls of plastic card faced with embossed stone plastic card. The slate roofs were covered with overlapping strips of thin card cut to represent individual slates. The wooden extension at the front of the building has walls of balsa scribed with a burning-pen to simulate planking. This section was roofed with corrugated copper. The windows are from Airfix kits.

will involve cutting round the window or door in question and bending it outwards or inwards.

With the basic walls complete and after adding any interior walls, floors and details which you want, the roof can be fitted. The basis of the roof is cut from card, wood or plastic card as for the walls. On this is applied detailing to represent the roofing materials. Slates and tiles are most simply modelled by applying an appropriate commercially-produced slate or tilepaper. This is glued on as with brick and stonepaper, but usually without the complication of openings unless there are skylights or dormer windows. Faller include slate roofing, and small and large tile roofing in their range of coloured embossed card sheets and these give a more realistic texture then the ordinary slate and tilepapers.

An even better effect is achieved by applying

Realistically modelled thatched cottages at the rear complete this scene on the 4 mm scale 'Pipers Mead' layout constructed by Allan Downes. Note also the damaged roof of the engine shed and the workman about to climb up the ladder to repair the hole. Small details like this add greatly to the realism and interest. (Photograph by John Priest.)

individually modelled tiles or slates cut from thin card or plastic card. However, this process is rather laborious and a good compromise which gives a very similar appearance with much less work is to use strips of tiles or slates. Each strip is cut a little longer than the roof length and twice the visible tile or slate height in width. Cuts are made half-way across each strip from the lower edge at intervals equal to the width of the tiles or slates. These sections between the cuts represent the individual tiles or slates. Broken or missing tiles can be simulated by cutting part of the card away. To tile a roof start at the lower edge and glue a strip of half the width of the tile strips along the roof. Then fix one of the tile strips on with its lower (cut into) edge along the lower edge of the roof. Then work upwards gluing strips on with each strip overlapping the upper half of the one below until you reach the ridge at the top of the roof. Do the same on the other half of the roof. Then fit a capping strip, also of card and folded along its centre, to complete the roof. Painting and weathering is then carried out.

A little time can be saved if we take a short cut by using a commercial slate paper and glue it down on to thin card for use in cutting up into strips for roofing. The printed lines on the paper are then a guide and we do not need to measure the strip widths and slate spacings.

Corrugated iron roofs are simply modelled by cutting commercially available copper or aluminium into scale-sized sheets and gluing them on to the roof. For tar-paper roofing I use paper tissues glued down, with a few wrinkles, and then painted black or very dark grey.

Thatch is more difficult to model. Pendon Museum at one time used human hair but this was very expensive and had to be specially mothproofed, so they now use plumbers' hemp, available cheaply from ironmongers, instead. This is glued down with PVA in bundles, arranged much as in real thatching, and is then painted. Allan Downes uses thick knitting wool glued on to a shaped roof. The wool is then brushed with 'Resin W' and flocked with an earth mix texture. As the glue dries it contracts and draws the flock into the strands giving a realistic thatch appearance. Examples of thatched cottages built by Allan Downes can be seen in one of the accompanying pictures. Another alternative method is to use modelling clay textured with a modelling knife to give the surface appearance of thatch and then painted.

Chimneys show a wide variation in style and type and it is a good idea to observe these and to make notes, sketches and photographs as a record to which you can refer when modelling. Chimneys are conveniently made from wood cut to size and shape. Brick or stone chimneys can be modelled with the same surface finish as used for the rest of the building as described earlier. Used ball-point refills provide tubing suitable for the chimney pots.

As you gain experience in scratch-building you will come across new methods and materials and new applications of ones already used for other purposes. Such experimentation is an enjoyable and rewarding part of this type of modelling.

Interior modelling

Whether or not to provide interior details for structure models is largely a matter of personal preference, partly influenced perhaps by the size of your layout and the number of model buildings there are on it. Many modellers feel it is a waste of time and effort to fit them as so little, if any, of the interior is visible, particularly in the smaller scales, once a building is placed on the layout. Others like to make the interior as fully detailed as the exterior and may arrange for the roof or one wall of the structure to be removable so that the inside of the building can be seen properly. Several American modellers have carried out very fine work of this type with structures which are exquisitely detailed both inside and out and certainly for success in the major competitions in the United States full interior details do seem to be necessary! In this country some of the best examples of interior modelling in 4 mm scale must be the model buildings in the Pendon Museum. One of the interiors is complete right down to a stuffed owl in a case, a wireless set with headphones and even pairs of socks drying in front of the fire!

Interior fittings are not for the most part included in kits though some of the craftsman type wood structure kits produced in the United States do include full details permitting the construction of a model of exhibition class, as can be seen in the Fine Scale Miniatures rail car shed kit. I am not aware of any parts made in Britain for interior detailing in the usual railway modelling scales though, of course, a selection of excellent items are available for military modelling in 54 mm scale. In the United States a remarkably complete range of furniture and other interior detailing models in the form of white metal castings are produced in HO scale by Scale Structures Ltd. This manufacturer offers furniture of all types, staircases including a fine spiral stairway, office equipment, a carpenter's bench and tools, bathroom fittings, even a barber's chair and pool tables, as well as smaller parts such as books, bottles, jars and musical instruments! Also in the range are wallpapers, curtains, paintings, rugs and carpets all printed in full colour. There is also a beautifully detailed selection of workshop machinery including a lathe, power saws of various types, a planer, a milling machine, a wheel grinder and a jointer, all accurate models of real equipment and ideal for a factory or machine shop model. With the excellent models made by this firm full interior detailing can easily be added to any structure of American prototype. These parts may be available in Britain from one of the specialist suppliers but they are quite expensive.

Furniture, machinery and other items for modelling interiors can also be made from scratch using scraps of wood, card and plastic together with odds and ends from the scrap

A fascinating historical model by Thorp Modelmakers Ltd of a cathedral interior showing how construction work was carried out. (Photograph by courtesy of Thorp Modelmakers Ltd.)

Because of their large windows and often prominent positions on model railway layouts it is worth while fitting interior detailing in signalboxes even if this is not done for other buildings. This 4 mm scale cabin is largely scratch-built but the windows and stairs are parts from an Airfix kit. Interior details include the levers, table, chair, sink and a clock and track diagram on the wall, all easily made from scrap materials.

box. Unless you plan to make the interior accessible for viewing and want full interior details these models can be relatively simple. If seen only through the windows the fittings inside need be little more than simple shapes suggesting the furniture or machinery within.

Generally a compromise between an absence of any interior fittings and full detailing will probably suit most modellers. It is desirable to include at least some interior walls and floors of card, wood or plastic card, in model buildings to avoid the appearance of an empty shell. If the structure has large windows and is near the front of the layout it is worth adding at least simple interior details. Signal boxes which face the onlooker need interior fittings as the large and numerous windows make the inside clearly visible. It is also essential to dress up the windows of shops with suitable goods. If you find that you enjoy this aspect of modelling you may want to go further and add as much detailing as you can. Knowing that a model building is fully detailed inside as well as outside can be very satisfying to the modeller. If you have only a small layout with space for very few structure models, detailing the interior will prolong the enjoyment of construction and will also improve the standard of your models. If you do model the interior fully it is best to arrange access, usually by having a removable wall or roof, so the details can be displayed to full advantage.

If there is interior lighting some interior fittings will often be needed and conversely if you have modelled details inside the structure you may well want to include lighting to make these more visible. Such lighting can be provided with 'grain of wheat' bulbs and these may be necessary if the bulbs themselves will be visible, as may be the case if the interior is fully modelled. However, it is more economical to use larger bulbs, either torch bulbs or, even better, the low-consumption 14-volt bulbs. If these are run at a lower voltage they will last very much longer. The light output will be reduced but this is of no consequence and may even be more realistic. These larger bulbs should be installed so that they illuminate the interior without being visible themselves. One method is to fit the bulb underneath the building and to make shafts from card so that the light only reaches the places in the building where it is required.

A most interesting recent development is the application of fibre optics to modelling. In this system light is transmitted along the fine glass or plastic filaments making up the fibre, which can be bent around curves if necessary. In a model, light can be transmitted along these fibres from a bulb or bulbs beneath the structure or under the baseboard to situations where there is insufficient space for even the smallest 'grain of wheat' bulb. The transmitted light is emitted at the end of the fibre as a pin point; if the tip is slightly melted to make it more bulbous a good representation of a very tiny light bulb is obtained. Fibre optics can be used to light rooms in a model building; even table lamps and standard lamps can be modelled if desired. It is also possible to light small signs; by positioning a rotating disc with holes in it between the light source and the fibres these signs can be made to flash on and off. With appropriately arranged holes and several fibres, lights can be made to go on and off in a pre-set order. The potential of fibre optics for lighting model structures is almost unlimited and the modeller may find some experimentation rewarding. One source of fibre optic materials and parts for modellers is Makemass Ltd of Crayford in Kent.

Low relief models

The modelling of structures at the rear of a model railway layout or military diorama in low relief is an ingenious solution to two problems which confront the modeller. One is the lack of space available to most of us for our layouts; low relief models occupy much less area than corresponding conventionally modelled buildings, a considerable advantage. The other problem is the difficulty of making a two-dimensional backscene look realistic when it can be viewed from a wide range of positions; scenes drawn in perspective to give an impression of depth are only correct for a very limited viewpoint and, when viewed from other positions, there will be distortion which spoils the effect. If low relief structures are employed the flat backscene need only be a simple sky blue background or one of the commercially-produced sky and cloud sheets.

Low relief buildings have the fronts fully modelled but are only an inch or so deep so that only the front parts of the sides and roof are constructed. This full modelling of the fronts means that they can have proper detailing giving a depth and texture which cannot be achieved with a two dimensional backscene. The fact that the buildings are not complete can be disguised by adjacent structures or by trees or other features.

Several manufacturers have realised how useful these models are to the military and railway modeller and have included examples in their ranges of kits. There are several models in the 00-scale Superquick series and in 00, TT and N scales in the Hamblings Bilteezi range. Builder Plus also now offer some kits of this type. These kits are all printed card models but Midland Model Railway Supplies make a range of vacuum-formed plastic mouldings including low relief scenic backgrounds and low relief buildings in 00 and N scales.

It is also possible to modify ordinary kits for

These three 00-scale structures were built from one of the Superquick low relief kits. The models have a realistic appearance but the depth is only about 1¼ in.

A very effective low relief factory on an 00-scale layout built by members of the Poole & District MRS. The model is a conversion from Builder Plus factory kits.

use as low relief models. This has the advantage that the front and back can be used separately so that each kit will provide two models instead of only the one. You may need to add some extra parts or details to complete the models. Alternatively you can, of course, scratch-build low relief structures giving you complete freedom of choice of prototype. Thus you can select buildings which are appropriate to the locale. The usual methods and materials are employed in construction but the models will be much quicker to build as only the front and part of the sides and roof need be modelled. Whether the models are kit- or scratch-built remember that if there are any windows or open doors the interior of the model should be painted black so that the viewer cannot see that the model has very little depth. If desired, interior lighting can be fitted. Interior fittings can also be included if the modeller wishes. If the low relief models are shops the windows should be detailed with appropriate goods on sale.

It often gives a good effect if a row of low relief buildings are modelled so that some extend a little further forward than others. This variation will give a more natural and realistic appearance and it also enhances the illusion of depth. When modelling a row of low relief buildings it is generally best if they are all approximately the same height. If not then the lack of depth of the structures which are higher is more apparent and tends to spoil the effect.

Low relief models are not only very useful from the purely scenic point of view but are also valuable for concealing hidden sidings or tracks, or a fiddle yard. In these circumstances it may be desirable to arrange for the buildings, preferably as a unit, to lift off the layout to provide easy access to the hidden tracks when necessary.

Painting, weathering and lettering

These finishing touches for a model building, or indeed any type of model, are very important in achieving a realistic appearance. No matter how skilfully you construct a model a poor paint job can spoil all your previous efforts. Conversely a very ordinary model can be made to look very good by expert finishing. Thus it is well worth while making an effort to become good at this aspect of modelling. Practice is probably the most important factor but I hope that some of the comments which follow may also be helpful.

The card kits are printed in full colour and apart from a little touching up, particularly of the cut edges, painting is not usually required. Wood kits can be painted if desired, using model paints such as Humbrol, but often staining gives a realistic and natural finish. When assembling these kits a little glue almost always gets on to the wood around the joints and even if it is wiped off immediately a trace is likely to remain. As the stain will not take over glue there will be pale marks at these places. It is therefore a good idea to stain the wood sheet and strip before assembly. These are various wood stains available from DIY and paint shops which can be employed. Alternatively I have used a thin wash of brown/black model paint effectively on wooden buildings, such as the gold mine shown in one of the photographs, to give a natural weatherbeaten wood appearance.

The metal kits should be primed; I find the Duplicolor automobile grey primer in aerosol cans convenient for this. After the primer has dried the models can be painted with ordinary model paints of appropriate colours.

Many of the plastic kits have their parts moulded in suitably coloured plastic to make painting unnecessary. In many cases the appearance without painting is quite good especially if the models are weathered to tone down the colours a little and to introduce some variation in tone. However, most plastic surfaces have a slight sheen and do look like plastic rather than the construction material they are supposed to represent, and good painting will give a better finished appearance. On the other hand a poor paint job will probably give a result which is inferior to the original unpainted plastic!

Because the gloss paint used on real buildings soon becomes dirtied and loses some of its shine from deposits of dust and grime and from the effects of rain and sunshine, and because the distance at which we view our models is equivalent to looking at real structures from much further away, we need to paint our models with matt and not gloss colours. Another good reason for doing this is that a gloss finish will show up every little

A small gold mine in HO scale scratch-built in balsa sheet and stripwood. The model was constructed following an article by an American modeller, Earl Cochrane, published some years ago. A weathered effect was achieved by painting the wood with a thin wash of black and brown paint.

imperfection whereas a matt paint will obscure these faults. Because there are no reflections a matt finish shows up details better and more clearly than gloss paint does.

Several manufacturers offer suitable ranges of paints. Humbrol is one of the best-known makes and I usually use these paints but there are others which are equally suitable. These paints are also fine for wood and card though for these materials I often use poster colours, such as those made by Winsor & Newton or Rowney. These paints are easy and convenient to use and have the advantage of being water-based. Whatever paint you are using, a dark grey will give a better appearance than a pure black for parts which in the prototype are black. It will also make small details more visible. Humbrol include a Dirty Black in their range but you can also add a little white and perhaps a touch of brown to the ordinary black for a similar result.

I have already mentioned that it is often easiest and neatest to paint some or all of the parts of a model before or during assembly rather than after the structure is complete, particularly if various parts are to be different colours. For buildings with more complicated paint schemes or lettering it is very convenient if construction can be arranged so that the walls can be fully modelled, painted and lettered before they are fitted together to make up the building. In this way the painting and lettering can be carried out with the sides flat on the workbench making the task much simpler. A little touching up may be required after assembly but this is not difficult if most of the work has been done beforehand.

For brush painting you will need a selection of different sizes including a very fine brush for small parts and details. Always buy good quality brushes. Though they are more expensive they will last longer and will not shed their hairs as you use them. They will also give a superior finish. Never apply more paint than is needed; excess will merely obscure detail and fill in corners. Many of the good paints now produced will cover well with only one coat of the darker colours. For the lighter colours a further coat or coats will be needed. If a single thin coat is not covering properly do not try to put the paint on more thickly as this will give a poor finish, very likely with blobs and runs. For the best results flow the paint on smoothly from the brush, covering the whole surface quickly and evenly without going back to apply more paint or to rebrush areas already done. Then leave the model for the paint to dry thoroughly and apply a second coat after that if necessary. Do your painting in a dust-free spot away from where you do your sawing, filing and sanding. Bedrooms are also to be avoided as there is usually a good deal of dust from bed clothes. Always clean your brushes thoroughly after use. A good method is to clean them first in the appropriate thinner or solvent and then follow this with a wash in warm, soapy water. Rinse and dry them before putting them away. The brushes should be stored so that they are not standing on the bristles and so that they will not be damaged.

The best results of all can be achieved with an airbrush. For long a tool only for the professional worker there are now a number of airbrushes on the market intended especially for the amateur modeller. They are still quite expensive but if you do a reasonable amount of model painting the outlay can be worth while for the convenience and for the excellent finish which an airbrush can give.

Lettering is always difficult to do well by hand unless you are a skilful draughtsman, particularly when working in the smaller scales. Dry print lettering from the Letraset, Blick and other ranges can be the answer to this problem. If you do your own photographic work you can produce perfect lettering and signs to any required size or scale by photographing either the original full-size sign or a sign hand drawn or made up with dry print lettering to a larger scale, for ease and neatness, and then printing the resulting negative to produce a sign of exactly the size you want for your model. Once the original has been photographed it is, of course, easy to print as many copies as required so there is no difficulty in providing numerous identical signs for your own buildings and also for your friends.

There are also some excellent commercially-produced signs, notices and posters on the market. Many of these have been photographically reproduced from original signs and advertisements. Dart Castings, for example, offer a selection of railway posters in 2 mm and 4 mm scales which are from posters preserved in the Uplands Railway Museum, Bristol. Builder Plus have a large sheet of advertising signs and posters in full colour and suitable for use for N, 00 and 0 scales. A few of these colourful posters will add greatly to the interest of an otherwise blank wall. If appropriately selected they will also help to set the period of the scene. Notices and signs for use on railway buildings are also available commercially from various manufacturers. Chris Leigh, for example, produces a very neat set of etched brass GWR notices for 4 mm scale.

Some modellers, particularly in the United States, enjoy making up amusing names, often

Two views of a 4 mm scale model railway layout constructed by G. Iliffe Stokes showing some of his superb model buildings. Note particularly the selection and grouping of the structures to give a natural and authentic appearance. Excellent weathering also adds greatly to the realism of the scene. (1st view by J.H. Russell, 2nd view by John Himmens.)

involving a pun, for the shops, factories and firms on their layouts. Again, this is a matter of personal preference and others do not regard the idea with favour. For myself, I must admit I enjoy these little touches with names such as the 'Lee King Pipe Company' and the 'Term Oil Co' (the latter being an industry on the layout built by American modeller, Art Curren). The idea is not new. I can recall that the late John Ahern had 'Quibble & Cuss' estate agents, on his famous 'Madder Valley' layout in pictures taken in the 1940s. A favourite of mine is on a factory model constructed by another American modeller, Earl Smallshaw. The firm is the Miracle Chair Company and the slogan reads 'If It's A Good Chair It's A Miracle'!

Full-size structures do not appear newly painted for long and, if your model is to look like the real thing, a little weathering to simulate dust, grime, mud, rust and spillage must be applied. This weathering not only make the building model more realistic but also enhances its appearance by making details more noticeable and by giving the impression of distance. The further we are away from a real building the more dulled or muted and greyed the colours appear because of the atmospheric haze and fine dust particles in the air. Thus the application of weathering will help to make our model look more like the real building at a distance, than a small model seen close to.

The weathering can be quite light if the structure is supposed to be in good condition and well kept up, or heavy if you want to give the impression of neglect and disrepair. Take care not to overdo it, however, as it is easy to spoil the effect by too much dirt and rust thickly applied. The best guide is the real thing and colour photographs are very useful as a permanent record to which you can refer when actually painting your models. Various colours in the Humbrol range are suitable for dust, dirt and grime, and the selection includes Rust. These colours can be applied as they are, or as a thin wash. A dilute wash of grey or black will give an overall dulling or toning down of the original colour. Powder poster paints are also useful; they can be dusted on and then most of the powder brushed or blown off. Some will remain, more if the brush used is slightly damp, giving the appearance of dust or dirt. Applying more water on the brush will cause streaking, simulating the results of exposure to rain and wind. An airbrush is very useful for weathering as it is easy to apply a light overspray of paint giving a very realistic appearance. Oil spillage on storage tanks can be simulated with a little black gloss paint. Clear gloss varnish can be applied to give the appearance of damp areas due to water leaking from pipes or tanks.

Final details

When your structure model is complete some attention should be paid to its setting on the layout. If the model is just set down on top of the surface of the scenery there will almost certainly be unsightly gaps and cracks between the bottom edges of the walls and the ground, which can completely ruin the effect. After fixing the building down, a little plaster or filler should be used to fill in these gaps. When dry, touch this up with earth colour. If there are to be grass and weeds around the structure, apply a little glue along the ground against the bottom of the walls and sprinkle on green scenic dressing. If the building is to be rather neglected, glue can also be applied to the lower parts of the walls before the scenic dressing is put on, so that the effect will be of grass and weeds growing up the walls. Creepers on the walls can be modelled in a similar way, with the stems drawn in with paint or ink. On the structure models for the Pendon Museum the walls extend at least 3 cm below the ground level and the buildings fit into recesses left in the surface of the scenery. This is an excellent arrangement because the joins are much less noticeable than when a building is set on top of the ground and are also easier to conceal giving a very realistic effect of structures which have proper foundations.

Because the setting for a model building is so important in enhancing its realism we should pay almost as much attention to detailing the immediate surroundings as to the construction of the model itself. Often structure models will be placed in relatively inaccessible positions on model railway baseboards making it very difficult to work on these details. An excellent solution to this problem is to provide structure models with their own small bases, either for single

Terry Jenkins built this 4 mm scale country pub using 1 mm thick card for the basic structure. This was covered with Builder Plus sandstone paper on the walls and chimneys. Individually laid tiles were cut from paper. The model was mounted on its own base for neatness and convenience. It can easily be fitted on to a layout later as a unit.

Another public house modelled by Terry Jenkins again in 00 scale. Terry used embossed stone pattern plastic card for the walls in this model but construction is otherwise similar to that for the model in the previous picture.

buildings or, where convenient, for groups of models. The structure, or structures, can be fixed on to this base and all the necessary modelling and detailing of the immediate surroundings can be carried out with the unit still on the work bench. The small unit can be turned around to allow complete access to all parts and the modeller can benefit from the convenience and comfort which will not only make the job more enjoyable but will also permit him to do his best work. It is usually easy to fix the whole unit on to the baseboard when it is complete and its edges can be concealed by applying a little extra plaster at the join. One of the accompanying photographs shows a 4 mm scale model of a country pub built by Terry Jenkins and fitted on to a small base of its own on which the drive, lawns, walls and other details have been modelled. The whole unit can later be fitted on to a layout.

There are many small details which can be added to complete the scene. Fences and walls are needed, either commercially-produced

The realistic details in front of this building give a more authentic look to the scene. Note also the effectiveness of the numerous accurately modelled roof details on this 4 mm scale factory building constructed from scratch by Tony Butler.

The setting is very important if model buildings are to appear realistic. This superb scene is part of the 4 mm scale Pendon Parva model at Pendon Museum. Note the perfectly modelled fencing, hedge, grass and paths together with the accurate model of a ladies cycle standing against the wall of the house on the left. (Photograph by courtesy of Pendon Museum.)

items or made from scratch. The yards of industrial buildings are often littered with scrap wood, old crates, scrap metal, oil drums, barrels, dustbins, carboys, and rubbish. Many suitable items are available from manufacturers such as Merit. Airfix 00-scale military vehicle kits are a good source of scrap parts including nicely detailed wheels and gears. These are very effective as scrap when painted with rust and weathering colours.

Houses can be provided with detailed gardens which have lawns, bushes, trees, and plants. There are many other items which can be added including a greenhouse or cold frame, children's toys, swings and so on.

Human figures will add life to the scene and there are numerous figures available commercially both painted and unpainted. If interior detailing is added to your models you may want to have people inside as well as outside the buildings.